finding

more heart

PHILOSOPHICAL MEMOIRS, PROSE, and POETRY

by Steven Mayer

To

Linda Fuss
the love of my life
my sanguine muse

If you don't know the kind of person I am
And I don't know the kind of person you are
A pattern that others made may prevail in the world
And following the wrong god home we may miss our star.

A Ritual to Read to Each Other, William Stafford

Contents

REFLECTIONS

RECOGNITIONS

OLD FRIENDS

Preface

෴

Finding More Heart will invite you to think philosophically, to notice more of what adds meaning to your life experiences, to reflect deeply about them, and to write your stories. I refer to this process as *finding heart*. It focuses on that nearly inexplicable yet clearly indelible human experience when we intimately and authentically encounter and embrace what really matters in life. It sustains living a meaningful life. Our unique wondrous life!

There are three types of philosophical prose in this volume: memoirs, essays, and poetry. My memoirs are largely based on stories told by my father and maternal grandfather, recollected with my aging memory. My essays are intentionally short and provocative, condensed from more exhaustive philosophical essays. Lastly, my poetry is an effort to distill ideas and experiences in a more condensed form. They are presented within the themes of Roots, Reminiscences, Reflections, Recognitions, Reverences, and Realizations. Six years ago, my first volume *Finding Heart* was published. Since then, I have continued to write. Again, my writing may be serious and contemplative, or light and whimsical. It matters not.

What matters is *finding heart*. We may not be able to define it well, but we know it when we experience it. Seeking and finding heart requires discipline to look past the ordinary and discover the extraordinary, to seek philosophical high ground and ask hard questions, and to revere the beauty and wonder of human existence. My philosophical skepticism runs deep, but I endeavor to define myself as a *hopeful skeptic* who primarily embraces the rigor of science and philosophy, but is open, albeit with prudence, to mystical and religious experiences. *Finding More Heart* reflects this orientation.

I encourage you to read my book with the perspective that you, too, *find heart* and have your stories to tell. You, too, have a *voice*. Even if your writing ability is weak, I promise you that it will improve with time, practice, and competent editing. I cannot promise you that those closest to you will read what you write, only that there are others who will cherish your words. Most importantly, you alone will know that your writing matters

Note: In the early spring of 2014, we were enjoying a long weekend on the north Oregon coast. We mused about an old dream of living at the beach during our retirement years. We decided to buy a small beach cottage and transition to a simpler lifestyle. Our days are more relaxed now, filled with beach walks and easy conversations. We feel liberated by having so much less and enjoying so much more.

ROOTS

Roots

ॐ

(notes to my family)

There may be times in our lives when we become strangers to each other, you and me. Unnoticed doubts and fears may separate us, in ways less understood. Yet, these gaps can be bridged with authentic, trustful conversation, by sharing our deepest thoughts and feelings, and by remembering who we truly are at the core of our being.

There may also be times in our lives when we become strangers to ourselves, you and me. We may think we began when we were born. We did not. There is an immense historic and genetic endowment that has shaped us, in ways less imagined. We often fail to see this dynamic clearly. We are more than the present or future, more than you and I appear to be even to ourselves, more than our life as we know it. The core fibers of our being run deep into the past, connecting us with our ancestors. They are embedded in our character and personality. Beyond family history or genetic mapping, there is a stream of essence that binds us forever, lifts us into a fuller realization of our complete self, and propels us purposefully into the future.

High in a tiny village in the Carpathian Mountains of eastern Hungary (now Slovakia), near the end of the 19th century, a young boy herded sheep with his faithful dog. He often slept under the summer stars, dreaming of the new world of which his parents spoke. Unable to rise above the hardships of life, his parents sent him alone at the age of seventeen, across the breadth of Europe and across the Atlantic Ocean to America. They would never see him again. His was an incredible journey of hope. His life, self-taught in philosophy, music, mathematics, and carpentry, imprint your personality and character. They speak to you, without voice, inexplicably, indelibly. Listen. He was my grandfather, a good man who sacrificed and endured much, for love of family. His passion and intelligence flow within you today. Can you sense their presence?

In Ukraine (mid-19th century) in endless fields of grain, toiled a young maiden who sells her produce and flowers to a passing band of traders. She has bright eyes and a lust for life. She notices a young man who has traveled far from the great mountains to the east, leaving his home to find a better world. She helps him to regain his health for the journey ahead. They fall in love. They walk far for love, and labor hard, farming the land. Their strength is in your shoulders and legs, their toughness in your spirit, and their smiles in the brightness of yours. She dies in childbirth, giving a daughter to the earth, my great, grandmother. The dreams that they dreamt are in your heart, too. Can you see them? I see them, even know them.

A century before, a fisherman along the north shore of Turkey watches the sunset. A beautiful, young woman with dark hair and eyes from a nomadic tribe of gypsies, stops for rest, migrating from the mountains of Persia. He watches her dance around the campfire. She plays her string instrument, magically, smiling at him. He is smitten. He falls in love with her fire and heart. She falls in love with his strength and independence. They cross the straits below the Black Sea and wander west up the Danube River Valley, where they endure the hardships of a people without a home. They have profound love of family and passion for life. Can you see them full of color and hear them laughing and rejoicing in spite of life's hardships, speaking to us? They are our ancestors, our family. Their blood is in our veins, their marrow in our bones, their tissue in our skin, even their feelings in our heart. Can you feel them? I feel them! They are a part of me.

All flows from my mother's ancestry, but there is so much more. Four streams converge in your being from your grandfather. They flow from the past nearly halfway across the planet and are still alive in us today. Farmers who toiled the land, merchants who traveled far, public servants, business owners, teachers (including a professor of philosophy in Germany and another of mathematics in Switzerland), artists, musicians, and hundreds of men and women who once lived and devoted much to creating a good life. In a harsh world, they raise children with little resources, sacrificing, working hard, and living and loving well. Without them, I would not exist, I would not be me, and you would not be you. They are all still a part of us. You may not be able to remember them; however, remember my grandfather's stories and be grateful for the incredible legacy these ancestors have given you and me. Let us honor them with the lives we create. And in our quiet hours, let us thank them.

We may sometimes think that only the future is important, that such musing about the past is mere nonsense and benignly inconsequential. I hope not. Understand that as we taste the fruit of our lives, its sweetness flows from roots deep within us. It is wise to remember well and celebrate our origins, for it dissipates the darkness around us and shines a soft, warm light into our lives. We will be more centered if we remember them. It seems tragic to continue as we do, so void of the past in the present, for our future will be diminished by it, and we risk being strangers to ourselves, you and me.

Note: This prose was written primarily to inspire my family. Readers are likely to have similar stories to share and preserve. *Heart* is found by researching and telling these stories.

Looking Back

ﻌ

It was a simple two-story square building, that tavern in Lackawanna, New York. There were two windows on each side of the two bedroom second-floor apartment where the owner, Juhasz, lived with his family. His two, nearly grown, daughters shared a bedroom. The bar was on the first floor with few windows and doors. It was several blocks from the steel mill, and the workers stopped there after work for a drink or two or three. It was a rough, rowdy, dimly lit place with bar fights, gambling, and no music. Cheap whiskey was illegally distilled in the basement. A side "red light" entrance led up to a single second-floor room that was occupied by prostitutes on most evenings. Juhasz confined his two daughters to the family quarters on the second floor. They would be at risk in the bar. No trees or gardens were near the tavern, as it was surrounded by empty lots on three sides and a highway in front, across from railway tracks. There were no nice neighborhoods either, though a small park by Lake Erie was about a half mile away. It was not an ideal place to raise a family. His wife, Julia, was very unhappy, offset only by the enjoyment of her daughters.

On weekends, the girls would go to the park, enjoy the gardens, feed the birds, lie on the grass, and share their dreams for hours. It was 1906. Rose was twenty and her sister Elizabeth was seventeen. They were beautiful in the floral dresses their mother made them. On a summer day, a young immigrant man, Steve Chorey, walked by, noticed Rose, smiled, and started a conversation. Steve had come to this country from eastern Hungary, while Rose had already been here for a number of years from her home in Budapest. They shared a common language and culture. He was smitten. So was she. They agreed to meet at the park every Sunday and go for a walk, while the sister watched from a distance. Her father did not know about this boy, and her sister was sworn to secrecy.

My Mother and Grandfather at Rose's Gravesite

Rose became pregnant in 1907 and gave birth to a son, Andrew, in 1908. Her angered parents kept her and the baby confined to the apartment. There were no more walks in the park. Steve went to her home, walking the five miles from Buffalo, but was immediately rejected and threatened by Rose's father. Steve was beaten so severely in the tavern that he had to fashion a wooden tooth in his mouth. He was not ready to give up. He tried to get a job at the local steel mill and move closer, but he failed. After the baby was born at home, Rose would take him for walks in the park, and Steve would secretly meet her and see his son for the first time. Rose became pregnant again at twenty-five and gave birth to a daughter, Mary Rose (my mother), in 1910. Finally, her father agreed to allow Steve to visit sparingly. It is unclear when they married, but it was sometime around the birth of her second child. Details of the marriage and their time together are nonexistent.

After the marriage, Steve's father-in-law refused to help the couple in any way. He didn't like or trust Steve, and he certainly didn't want Steve interfering with his life. Steve took Rose and the two children with him to wherever he could find employment, mostly in Buffalo. Surviving was complicated because neither could speak English well. Rose would have three more children: Steve in 1912; Elizabeth in 1914, who was named after Rose's sister; and John in 1916. In early 1918, Steve was unemployed and went to Pittsburgh to work and see his brother who was returning to Hungary. Steve paid the rent in advance, but the landlord later demanded more rent from Rose. She asked her father for help; he refused and insisted that she move into the tavern's basement. It was cold and damp with two small windows. She developed pneumonia in 1918 and died at the age of thirty-two, leaving five small children with their father nowhere in sight and no family willing to care for them. Her father, over the objection of his wife and daughter, placed the children in different orphanages in the western New York State area. One child, Steve, was later returned, at the age of nine, having finished only the third grade, and lived and worked in the basement of the tavern, distilling whiskey for his grandfather.

Steve, the children's father, did not find out what had happened until he returned months later. Rose was gone and so were his children. Juhasz refused to provide him with information about Rose's death or the location of his children. The local police and Catholic church were of no help. It took him nearly a year to locate the children, but he did not have the means to care for them, so they remained in orphanages or foster homes. He was depressed and admittedly confounded. He located Rose's gravesite decades later.

As the years passed, Steve became a carpenter and moved back to Buffalo so that he could attempt to gather his family together. He eventually located all of his children and made efforts to see them. Andrew's childhood is unclear. The girls, Mary Rose and Elizabeth, were "farmed out" as indentured servants or housekeepers, and it took years to locate them. His son, Steve, entered the army at age seventeen in 1929, and he was mostly stationed overseas. His youngest son, John, whom he never knew well, drowned at the age of nineteen in the Niagara River in 1935. It was a hard time for reasons known and unknown. My grandfather, Steve Chorey, and Aunt Elizabeth personally held old man Juhasz responsible for the death of Rose, and the mistreatment of her children. Even so, Steve Chorey slowly acknowledged over his lifetime that he shared responsibility for this family tragedy. Later in life, due to Steve's efforts, the family members found each other and were able to establish bonds and enjoy family reunions.

Relations with Rose's sister, Elizabeth, were strained, and only Mary Rose had regular contact with her. Elizabeth married Steve Syakos and lived in Massena, New York, three hundred miles away. I would visit her during the summers of my youth and refer to her as Grandma. She would tell me these stories as would my grandfather.

My grandfather never had the opportunity to raise any of his children, leaving many unanswered questions as to why. This period in American history was very difficult for immigrants with no family support, resources, job skills, or language proficiency. Family dysfunction, disunity, and tragedy were common. It is also clear that Steve should have been more responsible, a dark reality that haunted him throughout his life. Later in life, as he gathered his children around him, he found some redemption. He also became the primary caregiver for Mary Rose's son, his namesake—me. He may have been a poor husband and father, but he was a wonderful grandfather. Love overcame pain in the end.

My Old Teacher

☙

When I was a boy, I struggled to read and write in English because of the many other languages spoken around me: Hungarian, Slovakian, Czech, Italian, and German. In third grade, I could mostly understand my teacher, but my learning ended there. My parents spoke English, but my maternal grandfather was my primary caregiver, and he spoke Hungarian, as I did in conversing with him and with several of my childhood friends. My neighborhood was a rich mosaic of ethnic differences, mostly of eastern European origin, nearly all second-generation immigrant families.

As a young boy, I was oblivious to the outside world. The merchants in neighborhood stores spoke English, but my neighbors spoke mainly Italian. All of these languages seemed quite normal to me; it was simply the way it was, and I didn't know any different. My grandfather would read to me in English but speak to me in Hungarian. During my third-grade year, I struggled to read and write at school, as did other kids from my neighborhood. The school principal informed my parents of my lack of academic progress due to language issues. My father and grandfather were determined to right the situation, and immediately, I became immersed in a crash home study course in learning to read and write English.

It was not enough for my grandfather to simply have me read my school books or newspapers to him. It was his mission to build my intellect by reading more advanced materials, with a dictionary by my side of course. New words came at me at a bewildering pace, many of which we memorized but could not pronounce. I would often show these words to my teachers to learn proper pronunciation. By fifth grade, I met with my grandfather every day after school to read from his select books. I have a fond yet painful memory of one of these books which was filled with interesting people and ideas, albeit extremely difficult to read, *The Story of Philosophy* by Will Durant, a historian. The book focused on the lives and opinions of the western philosophers. Plato, Aristotle, Spinoza, Kant, Schopenhauer, Nietzsche, and Russell became my intellectual playmates. Understand that it was not a simple read; rather, we read and reread pages, not only practicing English but also seeking understanding of their ideas. My grandfather would question me on what I read, ask for my opinions, and often require me to write down my thoughts, a task that was nearly hopeless in those early days.

I later discovered that my grandfather liked Durant because they were similar in age and shared a passion for philosophy. In addition to learning English, he instilled his philosophical passion in me, so I would "think cogently and logically." The summer after my sixth-grade year, my grandfather challenged me to read Durant's *Story of Civilization*, Volume One, titled *Our Oriental Heritage*. It was a thick book, but he paid me to read it and of course report my insights to him. The world was opening up to me, and my mind to it. The next summer brought Durant's Second Volume, *The Life of Greece*. I loved it, and it complemented the Latin studies in my Catholic catechism. My philosophical foundation was being laid, brick by brick, it seemed. I would read Durant's subsequent three volumes in the following years, before my grandfather tired of this effort (the fifth volume titled *The Renaissance* was my favorite). Will Durant had become my teacher. He was difficult to read, challenging my English. At the end of my seventh grade, I was awarded recognition for an essay, though honestly, my grandfather mentored me through it. It was also becoming clear that I thought more critically than other kids, but I still found the English language to be a formidable challenge, reflected in my "C" and "D" grades in English. Writing was the major problem.

After five volumes of Durant, my attention turned to other writers. My father was an armchair historian of the Revolutionary and Civil wars, so he also began to challenge me to read history. Life moved on, and Durant was left behind. Later in life, I discovered that he wrote six more volumes of the *Story of Civilization*. I purchased the-eleven volume set for my library, though it would take me years to finish reading them. It was always good to visit with my old teacher again.

The set of Durant's *Story of Civilization* remained in my library for forty years. In an effort to retire and simplify my life, I dismantled my library, giving books away, saying farewell to so many old friends. It was not easy, but very necessary. The Eugene Public Library took my Durant set, but I continue to sentimentally retain a copy of his *The Story of Philosophy* in my small library. I just couldn't say farewell to my beginnings, for his influence on my life.

Recently, I wandered into a local bookstore, promising myself not to buy a book. I discovered Durant's *Fallen Leaves*. He had died in 1981 without barely a mention of this final manuscript of personal essays. It was discovered thirty-years later by his granddaughter and published in 2014. I have read and reread it, much like I read him in my youth. His prose was even more sophisticated and compelling, so cogent and lucid. While I argued with several of his ideas, my old teacher spoke to me and warmed me with his presence. It was good to hear from him again.

Haunted by Rose

ॐ

Fantasy is a wonderful gift, as I watch my grandson play his guitar so incredibly well. His talent may flow from my Hungarian grandmother, Rose (Rozsa) Juhasz. As I sit back and listen, I imagine she is listening and smiling, too, with a few tears of joy.

She was already deceased when I was born. She lived in the memories of my maternal grandfather (her husband) and her younger sister Elizabeth, and as a boy, I would listen to their stories about her. One of those stories was how beautifully she played her string instrument to the delight of family and friends. Her favorite place, in true gypsy tradition, was to play in the evenings around a campfire. Both my grandfather and great aunt spoke about being carried away by her soft music, that it continued to haunt them in the quiet hours of their lives.

This instrument was in the possession of my grandfather who kept it locked in a long narrow wooden trunk in our attic (the trunk was further locked in a closet and the door up to the attic was also locked). He treasured it, and he would rarely show it to anyone. As a young boy, I was one of the few exceptions. Inside the trunk, it was carefully wrapped in colorful Hungarian cloth. He would unwrap it, and set it in my lap, but not without strong words of caution. Strumming the instrument, the sound was mesmeric. As I did, my grandfather wept.

He wanted me to play it someday, but abandoned hope when I failed miserably to learn to play the violin.

Decades later, when my grandfather died, I returned to Buffalo, New York for his funeral and was invited to say a few words about him. As I did, I mentioned Rose's instrument, and the mood became dark, as relatives informed me that it had been stolen. I have often wondered what happened to it, that perhaps it is in a museum or private collection somewhere.

I long to find it. I dream of finding it. I dream of hearing its sound again. Soft and melodic, yet played with gypsy vibrancy. Not the tinny sound of steel mandolin or bousouki. In my dreams, I do hear it, mystically, though I never heard Rose play it.

It was an intriguing musical instrument for a young boy to hold in his lap. It looked like a very strange guitar. It was finely crafted and made of beautiful variegated woods. It had a pear-shaped body, rounded in back, painted flowers around the face edges, and a rosette covered opening. It had 5-6 gut strings stretching up a long, narrow neck, topped with a carved ornate headpiece. In the early 1900s, Rose brought it to America from her home in Hungary.

In recent years, I have studied the history of Eastern European string instruments. I still have a vivid recollection of its design. Encouraged by a vibrant folk music tradition in most Eastern European countries today, and the wide range of instruments migrating from the past into the present, I hope someday to find an instrument identical to my grandmother's. Searching for one, I have identified the most similar ones with long-necked, pear-shaped 3-6 string designs: *saz (baglama)* in Turkey; *domra* in Russia; *kobza* in Ukraine; *cobza* in Romania; *tambura* in Bulgaria and Macedonia; *dangubica* in Croatia and Serbia; and *bousouki* in Greece. All of these plucked string musical instruments have many (but not all) of the features of my grandmother's. Missing is the hand painted flowered face design, 5-6 gut (or nylon) strings, and of course, the rosette covered opening. Such instruments are also found in the Middle East, North Africa, and Southeastern Asia. Given the history of my Hungarian family, and the likely migration of gypsies from central Asia, it is possible that my grandmother's instrument was indeed very old and may have been crafted along the migratory path. The wide-ranging presence of the *oud* in Arabia, Persia, North Africa, and Eastern Asia is evidence of a rich history of construction and migration of such wooden string instruments.

I have started a collection of such instruments (and my grandson Nathan can play them): a *bousouki* from Greece; a *baglama* from Turkey; and a *lute guitar* from Croatia. Having received advice from an expert specializing in Eastern European string instruments, I am likely to find a closer match if I wander the villages of southern and eastern Hungary in search of one. Such a pilgrimage is one of my fondest dreams.

I confess, but never as a boy in my Catholic confessions, that there were a few occasions when I snuck up into the attic, having "borrowed" my grandfather's keys from his dresser, and unlocked the trunk. Carefully unwrapping the instrument, I would pretend to play it.

I imagined Rose was there, too, teaching me. It became a romance of the heart in my youth. This memory haunts me still today.

Grandson Nathan Playing Eastern European Instrument

The instrument, while intriguing, is more about a different search, one to know my grandmother, Rose, and her Hungarian gypsy heritage. Each summer, as a young boy, I would travel about 300 miles to Massena, New York to visit my great aunt, Elizabeth (Erzebet), Rose's sister, for several weeks. She insisted I call her "Grandma." We would often take walks by the Saint Lawrence River, but never without her recounting stories of Rose. In her home. above her fireplace, was a portrait of Rose, dark hair and eyes, looking directly at me with a gentle smile.

Both the instrument and portrait are lost, but not in my heart.

Road Trip

 formula

During my youth in the 1950s, my father and I had a tradition of celebrating our birthdays together; they were in August, only four days apart. We would go on a road trip in our mint green 1948 DeSoto Coupe to visit my grandfather Mayer on his farm in Rome, New York, two hundred miles away. We would leave on an early Friday afternoon from our home in Buffalo, stopping at a small-town diner along the way. We took this road trip each year over a six-year period.

Arriving at the farm late, we would fall into bed but arise at the crack of dawn. We were going to watch our beloved Brooklyn Dodgers play baseball at Ebbets Field in the Flatbush neighborhood of New York City, another three hundred miles away. It was a long trip, but the miles slipped by as the horizon slipped forward. My mother never knew our true destination; she detested both road trips and baseball.

Sitting in the old stadium watching a Dodger baseball game was our birthday gift to each other. My dad paid for the tickets and I bought the hot dogs. At the age of six, I recall my father's enthusiasm when the Dodgers signed Jackie Robinson. When I took my first road trip at the age of nine, the Dodgers were the best team in the National League. I would stand near the home dugout, watching my favorite players: Duke Snider, Roy Campanella, Gil Hodges, Pee Wee Reese, and Jackie Robinson, hoping to get an autograph on my baseball glove. We always sat in the "bleachers," known as the cheap seats, waiting for a home run ball to come in our direction. If we were really lucky, they played their chief rivals, the New York Giants, in the "Subway Series."

As a kid, I suffered through numerous World Series losses against the New York Yankees. If that wasn't hard enough, after these series, older boys in my neighborhood who were Yankee fans would chase me and beat me up. They were among the first to wear World Series Champions shirts to school, rubbing the pain in deeper. "Wait 'til next year" was the typical response by Dodger fans. Not until the age of fourteen (1955) did the Dodgers finally beat the Yankees. Even so, if I celebrated too much, I would end up in fistfights.

Depending on game time, we would stay in New York City and rise early on Sunday to drive back to my grandfather's farm, traveling north up the Hudson River Valley and west along the Mohawk Valley. Sometimes, we would cut through the Catskill Mountains or south to the Finger Lakes. My father loved country back roads he had never driven down, singing along with old songs on the radio. We arrived back in Buffalo late Sunday night, exhausted and happy. A long memorable birthday weekend!

This story isn't about baseball. It pays tribute to a father-son relationship, and the memories created by it. We spent three long days of driving together, time to talk about baseball for sure, but more importantly, time to talk about life. My father didn't like "small talk." He would tell me that he was going to ask some tough questions, and he wanted me to think about them for a while before responding. There were questions about favorite topics in school and why, best friends and why, favorite books and why, favorite places and why, and so forth, with emphasis on the "why." Of course, he was "warming up" for tougher questions: What do you think is important in life? What do you think you will do with your life? What do you think about a particular issue or situation? What do you think about religion? What do you think about the philosophical stuff that Grandpa Chorey is putting into your head? These conversations would last for hours.

If I grew weary, he would share his most inner thoughts and feelings with me. Sometimes, it was about events in history books he had read or about his experiences as a labor activist. He loved telling stories, and he encouraged me to tell mine. He was a gentle man with tremendous passion for social justice and with little patience for nonsense. There were also quiet times as we drove along, enjoying the rolling green landscape, farmlands, and small towns. All my mother knew was that we visited grandfather Mayer's farm; no more, ever. This was a solemn oath we never violated.

I knew deeply that my father loved me, and wanted me to have a memorable experience on my birthday. As I grew older, a different tradition became part of my life: every year before I celebrate my birthday, I celebrate his in some way he would have enjoyed. In my mind, we have conversations about the "old days" and the good times we had together. I even dream about being with him back on the road again.

Talking to You Again

ॐ

Sitting here in my favorite chair
on a dark stormy winter night
listening to classical music
preparing my last term class, I
glance at your framed picture
notice you smiling at me.

I miss your presence in my life
your premature death haunts me
though you quietly listen still, I
share my life's incredible journey
my greatest love, joy, heartache
feel your arm around me again.

I lay down my class notes
accept your invitation to converse
bring you back into my presence
see you clearly, your gentleness,
hear you speak wisdom softly
to me again.

I want you to know, I
learned a few things finally, you
patiently tried to teach me.

Questions, reflections matter,
philosophy matters, living
life ultimately matters.

Thank you, Father.

Even when I am shaken, your
compassion sustains me.
When I am jubilant, your
humility quiets me.
When I am alone, your
grace, humor find me.

Thank you for your life, for
the life you have given me.
You are with me
always.

My Father: Anthony Mayer 1904-1958

My Father's God

ભ

My father was fond of saying, "God blesses us in ways we don't expect." His untimely death convinced me otherwise. If there was a God who indeed blesses us, then how do we explain needless suffering and evil in the world. Years later, I visited my old New York neighborhood and was reminded of my father's good works for others. The rage in my being was lifted unexpectedly. Consequently, I am fond of saying that my father's God blessed me in ways I didn't expect.

There are several ways to think about this borderline mystical experience. One is to embrace my father's view of a supernatural deity intervening in our daily lives to save us from ourselves. Though a practicing Catholic, his view of God was lovingly personal and present, albeit mysterious and unpredictable. If he had accompanied me on my walk through the old neighborhood, he would assert that his God was subtly revealing himself to me through his good works, and He was indeed present and attentive to us. I could feel the power of his belief in his virtuous life, though he seldom articulated it, much less advocated it. His life was one of pure example. His quiet reverence during a church mass was no different when watching a sunset or stepping back from doing a good deed.

My view is very different from my father's. The existence of God is doubtful, in my mind. I often borrow from the poet, William Stafford, who reminds us that we may "follow the wrong god home" because of patterns in our culture. To me, one of the wrong patterns resides in more radicalized religious beliefs and practices around us. I choose to think of the "right god" as a virtuous life. I openly confess to feeling closest to "God" when I sat on our front porch steps with my father as a boy, recounting all of the good deeds we did for people in our neighborhood. My father's premature death led me to disbelieve in God. That deep skepticism flows in my bloodstream until this day, but it does not overwhelm my emergent hopefulness to engage in good and kind acts. In my view, my father's god is not defined by what he believed, but by his willful acts of kindness percolating out of a virtuous life. His life radiated in the old neighborhood twenty years later, from the fences, window boxes, porches, and garages he built and we painted, and from the gardens and shrub beds he planted and we tended. Those memories lifted the rage from my being, not some abstract theology or worship rite. I saw clearly that my father followed the right god home by being a good person.

My atheist grandfather would smile, asserting that moral philosophers have wandered through the maze of what constitutes "the good life" for three thousand years, and that my father began and ended with Aristotle, that virtue is the core of a good life. Talk of categorical imperatives, utilitarian considerations, moral calculus, ethical relativism and pragmatism, and similar ethical assertions of religious and mystical traditions, fade into nonsensical prolixity and meaninglessness. My grandfather would simply assert that my father discovered what made him happy by helping others and embracing the flow of goodness into and out of his being. My grandfather held a different ethical perspective, but he would endeavor to question my father to clearly articulate his philosophy of life in a meaningful way. A gift well intended, but not one that my father valued. He had no need to "think" about his philosophy, only to live it.

I enjoy the philosophical legacy of my family, for it resides in me, grounded in my skepticism of truth claims, and in my compulsive obsession with ethical issues, ultimately sourcing my hopefulness in *finding heart* in the human condition. My grandfather's philosophers speak to me:

"If you would be a real seeker of truth, you must at least once in your life doubt, as far as possible, all things." Descartes, *Discourse on the Method*

"The unexamined life is not worth living." Socrates

"We cannot escape the issue of remaining skeptical and waiting for more light." William James, *The Will to Believe*

"Religious ideas (fulfill) the oldest, strongest, and most urgent wishes of mankind." Sigmund Freud, *The Future of an Illusion*

Now, in the end, it was my father's turn to smile, and be dismissive of my grandfather's insistence on the need for philosophical analysis. Life was much too important to not live it. Spend more time in action and less time in thought. Thinking about it was mostly irrelevant to what really mattered. And so, my father's god continues to bless me in ways I don't fully expect.

Note: For further historical background, see His Smile, *Finding Heart* (2012).

Memories on a Cold Wind

ॐ

It's another dark, rainy Friday evening in western Oregon. Heading home after work, my taste buds speak to me from my deep Catholic roots: *fish & chips!* There is nothing quite like some beer battered fish and fresh cut potato fries, with malt vinegar, sea salt, and tartar sauce. I adjust my route, giving in to the urge. Sitting at an outdoor cafe under an umbrella, I quietly enjoy my dinner while it is still fresh and hot.

A cold wind is blowing memories back to me, of growing up Catholic in New York State, and traditionally eating fish almost every Friday. Images haunt me of Buffalo's lower west side, and the 'all-you-can-eat' 50 cent fish fry at Joe's Place, situated near the Niagara River. I can still feel the wind off the river, and smell fish and beer in the air. The old diner, one of the community gathering places, was always packed full of neighbors. During dinner, there was live music, dancing, and an open mic for singers. Never dessert because everyone was too full of fish. After dinner, my father was inevitably drawn into a poker game and discussed the most recent Brooklyn Dodgers baseball games. My mother joined other women, sitting around the large, wrap-around porch, watching the sunset colors reflect off the clouds over Lake Erie. I played tag or touch football in a small playground with the other kids. Joe's Place had a certain mystique: a dumpy place with cardboard walls and sawdust on the dirt floor, even a leaky roof, never able to pass today's health standards. A place of the heart.

As I eat my cod or halibut fish dinner, I do so with ease. No bones. Not so lucky as a kid. Blue Pike and Yellow Pike (now extinct), plentiful in Lakes Erie and Ontario, were filled with bones, some so big that they could cause a serious problem if swallowed. My mother was a constant nag, warning caution with every bite, lest I choke to death. My father would invite me to compete with him to amass the biggest pile of bones. Speed was unimportant. Caution and bones mattered. My father ate slowly, and I did too, always winning, much later recognizing my father's cunning ways.

Whenever I feel the urge to eat fish on Friday, I morph into a New York Catholic again, from a poor blue-collar ethic neighborhood, full of foreign cultures, traditions, and languages. A beautiful place. I hear my father's laughter again. My mother's scolding, too. Music fills the air. Good memories surround me. It is a joyful haunt, rising up through layers of time. During my last trip to Buffalo's lower westside neighborhoods, I drove down to the Niagara River to find the diner. Nothing looked the same. Joe's Place was gone as was the small park. Loss filled me. But on a cold wind, I could still smell fish and beer. I closed my eyes, took a deep breath, and smiled again.

Confluence

ॐ

Sediment grows
in the midst of confluence
rising over time with
sustaining sentience.

These gentle streams
meandering along, narrowing
steadily, joining quietly
nearly unnoticed.

Walking along the banks
one flows from my beginnings
its current deep within me
strong in its power.

I wander upstream
kneeling to cup
water in my hand
to taste its history.

Stones overturned
are memories of
nearly forgotten time
haunting in their call.

His face smiles at me
reflected by the water's edge
a peaceful eddy reveals
his enduring presence again
its ripples, his soft laughter
its purity, his buoyant spirit.

My life is a confluence
unnoticed mostly
revered lastly, finally.

Along the second stream
I flow with her presence
visible, strong, vibrant
in every moment of my life.

Caught in its steady current
her hand tightly takes mine
rapids reveal her easy laughter
sounds of water, her song
fragrances of flora along her bank,
her kindness and grace in me.

REMINISCENCES

My Mormon Experience

ೞ

At the age of seventeen, I hitchhiked from New York to California to pursue a new life. I found work quickly but had difficulty making new friends. I met a guy at work who invited me to play on his church basketball team. Later, at a church social function, I met some young people my age who were outgoing and friendly. The girls were cute, and the church even had Saturday night dances. They were *Mormons*. I thought that they were like the Quakers or Amish. Enjoying their family orientation and the absence of hard drinking and partying, I began attending church services, though I was mostly ignorant of their beliefs. My new friends also went to college, invited me to do the same, and introduced me to an academic counselor who was incredibly encouraging and helpful. He was a Mormon, too. After a year, I decided to become a Mormon.

I knew very little about Mormon history or doctrine, but that didn't matter to me. In my youth, I was a Catholic and went to confession, Sunday Mass, weekly catechism, and served as altar boy. My family, however, never took church doctrine too seriously. I later discovered that Mormons took their doctrine very, very seriously. While talk of prophets, visions, angels, and new revelations seemed incredibly farfetched to me, I remained silent, making a concerted effort to develop my new religious faith. In the process, I became conflicted and neurotic but continued to attend church and enjoy my Mormon friends. I truly loved these people! In the spring of 1962, I completed over two years of college, and was on the verge of being drafted into the military, most likely going to Vietnam to fight in a war I protested against. I explored the options of moving to Canada, or being a conscientious objector, but settled on being a Mormon missionary. I guess I needed to read the Book of Mormon.

Author as Mormon Missionary in Germany

I was fortunate to be sent to Germany for thirty months, allowing me to live in Europe, learn the German language, become immersed in their culture, and even attempt to build my faith. I traded my California tan, beach volleyball, and tennis for a white shirt, dark suit, and a set of Mormon scriptures. I experienced little culture shock in Germany, as it was like returning to my old NY neighborhood with all of its ethnic and language differences. There was, however, psychological shock in relating to other missionaries because of their condescending attitudes toward Germans. At the same time, efforts to win new converts to this American religion were strongly rebuffed. Many missionaries relaxed their efforts, though there were outstanding exceptions.

I started looking for opportunities to engage in community service. One was conducting a general Christian funeral for Germans who were refused a church service. I conducted over twenty-five funerals in small German villages. Unrecognized at the time, I gave German families a gift denied to my father. Another area of non-traditional missionary service focused on helping church members repair their homes and enhance their yards. As neighbors witnessed our efforts, it led to the beautification of villages. It was not only wonderful to experience this transition, but communities became friendlier toward church members who had been previously shunned. In one village, we created a local weekly market of farm produce, crafts and bakery goods that attracted outsiders, and helped the community to prosper further.

In spite of these enjoyable non-traditional missionary ventures, I had two pivotal troubling church experiences. First, when I visited the Mormon Temple near Bern, Switzerland, it reminded me of peculiar practices that seemed irrelevant to virtuous living. I just "didn't get it!" Second, a visiting Church authority shared a blatantly racist "divine revelation" in which less valiant people were designated by the darker color of their skin. I began sensing that there was a deeper doctrinal level at play. More importantly, I privately decided I no longer wanted to be a Mormon but would "honorably" complete my mission. In good conscience, I stopped writing to a Mormon girl in California whom I really liked, knowing that I could never fulfill her expectations of being a committed Mormon.

At the end of my mission in early 1965, I decided to go to BYU because it provided the fastest track for my degree completion. My decision to leave the Mormon Church was delayed. At the end of my first (Spring) term, I met Linda Fuss, fell in love, and we married that summer. Linda was a Mormon convert, too, but one who was enthusiastic about her new religion. Love can be blind! Sharing my reservations with her, she encouraged me to make a leap of faith. In March 1966, our daughter Christina was born. Her arrival further changed things. My private dream of returning to Europe for graduate education was rightly abandoned. After graduation, we moved to work in Michigan. Our son, Steven, was born there in 1967. Linda and I went to church together, hoping it would soften my skepticism about Mormon doctrine. This idea was a noble experiment which, despite genuine efforts, ultimately failed.

In May 1969, we moved to Minnesota. Our second daughter (third child), Julianne, was born there in 1970. We were relatively active Mormons during our five years in Minnesota, taking the "good" offered by the church, and leaving the "rest" without critical commentary. I discovered that, like most religions, Mormon history had its scars and blemishes, and Mormon theology had its flaws and nonsense. I attempted to openly discuss my doctrinal and historical research with church members, only to discover that most were uninterested. Scars and flaws didn't matter to them; faith and obedience did.

In March 1974, we moved to Oregon. Prior to the move, we agreed to raise our young family outside the Mormon Church, a decision that finally resolved a twelve-year inner philosophical conflict for me. I began teaching part-time at the University of Oregon. Life was good! I was free of the Mormons at last. It was not to last! Mormons found us again, and we were drawn into a vibrant church community, filled with young families like ours. It provided instant friends to our children and us. However, we were no longer in the "mission field," and the full weight of Mormon orthodoxy came crashing down upon me. I was miserable but willing to endure the pain for the sake of my young family. We built a home in the country in 1976, which provided a healthy distraction from church. However, Linda and I had become increasingly distant. The church culture was not helping either of us to be our best selves. We went to marriage counseling, and I agreed to support our family's church involvement, and she agreed to support my efforts to teach our children to be open-minded reflective thinkers.

Linda's focus on church activity deepened, and she held numerous important leadership positions. When she had Saturday meetings, the kids and I would take off to the beaches, mountains, or swimming holes. I entered the PhD program at the University of Oregon in 1983, and it provided a philosophically friendly environment, congruent with my values. Not only was I a political liberal in a conservative church, but I viewed most of the men in the church as sexist and racist. In the end, the Mormon Church wanted me to be someone I did not want to be, and they could not accept me for the person I was.

My employment evaporated in early 1991, and I accepted a position with a new company in Portland. Over the next few years, we relocated to Portland and left the church. We were emotionally healthier without the Mormon religion in our life. We were more in love! For the past twenty-five years, I have not been a Mormon. I have no animosity toward the Mormon religion, as it provided tremendous support in my life; however, it was clearly incongruent with my personal philosophical views. When we left, we immediately lost most of our Mormon friends. So, we became challenged to develop new friends. We did so.

There is, of course, much more to this story. More details between the lines. More laughter and happiness along the way, and more heartaches and sadness. If I had to live my life over again, I would not have become a Mormon. I have no serious regrets, however, as I learned much about myself and what matters most to me.

Love Changes Everything

ℭ

I just wanted two research papers typed. It was nearing the end of my first university term at BYU, and I was overwhelmed with projects and exams. Good grades would result in a full-tuition scholarship which I desperately needed, given my limited resources.

I found a roommate of a co-worker to type my papers with the promise of completion by mid-week. Mid-week came and went with no papers. Contacting this girl was impossible! She was always out on a date. She, however, left a message that the papers would be typed soon. *Panic!* I attempted to retrieve my papers, only to be told that no one could find them. *More panic!* Finally, I contacted her on the day before the papers were due, and she told me to come over. I assumed to pick up my completed papers. *No such luck!*

When I arrived, she greeted me at the doorway, told me not to move, and went into the other room, hopefully, to retrieve my completed papers. She returned, having put on makeup and a different dress, with my untyped papers in her hand. *Not good!* She invited me in, set up her typewriter, and told me to sit next to her, so I could answer any questions. She typed very slow, and talked very fast, asking me about myself, and pointing out how much we had in common. And she was just a bit flirtatious. *Not good!*

I wanted my papers done, not a date. When I returned from nearly three years in Germany, I just wanted to finish my degree as expeditiously as possible and return to Europe to pursue a PhD in philosophy or mathematics. I already had a place in Cologne to live. Being back in the USA was a time for good judgment and common sense, not romance. I did, however, want to meet girls cautiously, deciding to date ten different girls during my first term. I was disciplined and on track, or so it seemed. It proved to be a minor delusion.

The papers took seven hours to complete; not the two hours, I expected. In the process, I enjoyed the company of this girl, so full of easy laughter and good humor. Maybe, I will ask her on a date sometime, but my papers were the immediate priority. We finally completed them. I left and I didn't give her another thought, until crossing campus four days later. She appeared out of nowhere, grabbed my hand and told me to go with her. Maria von Trapp ("Sound of Music") was speaking, and given my recent history, she thought I would enjoy it. Actually, I enjoyed her company more. Afterward, I invited her on a Saturday date. *I sort of liked this girl!*

We went to the movies, kissed, and the rest is history. We saw each other every day thereafter, and at the end of two weeks, we were engaged to be married. We both knew when it was right. We married six weeks later in California. We essentially eloped. Without good sense or resources, friends later set up a wedding reception for us, so we would have some dishes, silverware, and kitchen cookware. We lived in a cockroach-infested apartment, worked full-time, got pregnant, and returned to Utah to finish college "on a shoestring." We were in love, and love changes everything. No mention of returning to Europe ever. *Crazy!*

Most of our friends waited for the marriage to collapse, because we hardly knew each other and made an incredibly hasty decision to marry and start a family. The odds were against us, but love was on our side. Being both first born and willful children, we refused to fail. We grew to know each other and adapt to each other fully. Now, in our sixth decade together, we are still in love.

There is much detail between the lines, of course. There is little that we would change. Her blue eyes sparkle still when she looks at me, and that is enough.

Just Getting By

I can understand differences in people.

I can understand differences in perception and sensibility.

I can understand differences in opinion and values.

I can understand differences in personality and character.

I can understand differences in social and cultural reality.

I can understand these differences, mostly.

I can understand how such differences create

misunderstanding.

I can understand that my understanding is limited.

Understanding is no salvation from the pain of alienation.

I cannot understand the persistence of hate and rejection.

I cannot understand the extinction of patience and compassion.

I cannot understand the absence of kindness and forgiveness.

I cannot understand the presence of suffering and evil.

I cannot understand people who are in this dark space.

I can understand how misunderstanding persists.

I can understand how my misunderstandings confound me.

The lack of understanding aches my being.

I can hope to live life well in spite of this human condition.

I can hope for star-filled nights and new sunrises.

I can hope that time will heal us all in the end.

I can hope that love will redeem us in our quiet moments.

I can hope to hug and hold alienated loved ones again.

I can hope. I will always hope. I will never stop.

Heading North

ॐ

After I completed college in 1966, we moved to Michigan. One dark night, we took a shortcut home through an inner-city Ypsilanti neighborhood, and we were caught in an explosive race riot, damaging our car and nearly inflicting injury on us. Escaping harm, we returned home, shaken, but became even more unnerved when our neighbor wanted to return to the scene with a shotgun in hand.

The next day, at work, I was emotionally distraught, avoiding eye contact with my boss. He was a prominent black civil rights leader. He confronted me, and I shared what happened. He wept. He implored me to maintain perspective, to not give in to hatred. He shared his personal experiences with me for over an hour, stories of white and black racism. I wept, too. He loaned a Martin Luther King book to me, helping me to find my way back to sensibility.

After the incident, I noticed that whites and blacks seldom sat together in the workplace lunchrooms, reflecting perhaps a time when lunchrooms and restrooms were segregated. More disquieting was the large number of Confederate Flag bumper stickers in the company parking lot. Racial tension seemed to be just under the surface of daily living, inviting provocation. A year later, I witnessed a workplace incident of racial violence, resulting in fights, stabbings, hospitalizations, and arrests. It was terrifying to have a white foreman running toward me with a bloody pipe in hand, pursued by two black employees with knives. Once the incident was investigated by police, it was discovered that violence was provoked by a racially motivated physical assault toward a black employee. I was shaken again by racial outrage.

Our home in Michigan was in close proximity to a black neighborhood during the time of the Detroit riots. Black Panthers and KKK were both active in the shadows of life. White neighborhoods had been leafletted, threatening harm to white children. Blacks awoke to burning crosses and endured discrimination. Racial unrest was prevalent in the schools. Even so, my spouse taught part-time at an inner-city high school with an ugly reputation. She was admired by her students for her progressive teaching. They loved her and she loved them. Other teachers complained of disrespect, but not her.

We lived through the assassinations of Malcolm X and Martin Luther King. A truly tragic legacy of American culture blooded earlier by the assassination of John F Kennedy and later of Bobby Kennedy. All leaders promoted civil rights and were victims of racial hatred. I grew up in an inner-city neighborhood in upper New York State with an abundance of ethnic discrimination, but racial discrimination—white vs. black—seems so much deeper and more intense within most major US cities.

In 1969, we moved to Minnesota in an act of "white plight" to hopefully find a more peaceful environment. We later discovered that we had unwittingly sold our Michigan home to the Grand Dragon of the local Michigan KKK. He defaulted on our sale contract after going to jail for "tar and feathering" the high school principal where my wife had taught. It seemed to us that we were still fighting the Civil War over 100 years later. Perhaps it had never ended. I travel to foreign countries, only to find similar histories of racial bigotry and discrimination. Throughout the USA, I see media coverage of protests, though largely ignored in a society whose social consciousness is deadened by an ugly history, radicalized religion, and political apathy.

In Finding Heart, I shared an early childhood experience of racial bigotry in an essay, Heading South. Years Later, I discovered that the same bigotry was "Heading North." The stories shared in this essay are only a few of the incidents we experienced in California, Utah, Michigan, Minnesota, and Oregon. In my early practice of religion, I experienced blacks being denied the priesthood that only white males held. Segregation in religion, politics, and employment was common, an ugly endowment bestowed by a culture unchanged over time activated even in liberal-minded people on occasion.

I refuse to give in to racism. We are better than this. Much better! We need to get over it. We can learn from our history, purge our prejudices, and lift ourselves up into the clear light of social justice. Maybe.

Hope is a good thing, maybe the best of things!

Perfectly Happy Heart

ଓ

I am in love with a woman with a perfectly happy heart. Her heart is full of kindness toward others, usually a friend in need or someone less fortunate, more deserving of her spirit.

Staying up late into the night baking all sorts of cookies, I hear her humming to old songs on the radio. Love abounds. She dances and sings. Another huge box was sent off in the mail again today. She patiently longs for that special notecard or phone call, not just expressing thanks, but commenting on the taste, texture, and design of her creations. At the center of her kitchen is a perfectly happy heart.

Rising very early on another morning, she is baking cinnamon and orange rolls. Once baked and frosted, she is off to a local retirement center or homeless shelter to share her treats. And, of course, if a few street-corner panhandlers have their cardboard signs out, they may receive a treat, too. It is an expensive routine to stock up on flour, sugar, raisins, oatmeal, butter, eggs, and assorted spices, but she sacrifices other needs to cover the cost. Her gifts bring joy to others, brighten their day, and reaffirm that enough love is in this perfectly happy heart for all who cross her path.

Restless in the late evening, I discover the light on in her craft room. This woman is exuberant, creating an exquisite variety of Christmas or Easter cards from recycled materials. I wonder if anyone else in the world makes and sends such cards to friends. No matter; she will do so without even a thought of a response. It will brighten their celebrations, she exclaims. It is all so abundantly necessary, this perfectly happy heart.

Oregon Blackberry Picker in Heaven

Another day finds her picking up her 100-year-old mother to deliver brown bags of food and treats, prepared the night before, to street-corner homeless. These folks have come to recognize her mellow yellow VW Beetle convertible and call her by name. No matter if their begging is filled with ill motive; she is void of judgment. Their smiles are enough to add buoyancy to her perfectly happy heart.

She seeks her "pure heaven" in the late summer sun, deep in blackberry bushes. Spending hours pushing her way into the thorny interior, she searches relentlessly for the biggest and juiciest blackberries, balancing with a bucket in one hand and her walking stick in the other. She prays for just enough rain and sun to produce a vibrant harvest, best for the jam, cobbler, and pies. Unnoticed to others is the little girl I see, delighting in nature's bounty, coming out to play again. There is dance and song in her movement. On the breeze is a requiem of the heart.

When her oldest daughter decided to close her watercolor card business, this woman refused to recycle old inventory. Here was a legacy of creation, and it deserved to be shared with those who could appreciate her daughter's artistry. She spent countless hours repackaging cards with envelopes to distribute to retirement homes throughout Oregon. Never mind the expense of purchasing envelopes, it just had to be done. It was simply the right thing to do. Her perfectly happy heart was at play.

In the late autumn, another wonder is her brown-bag apple pie. Fussy in her selection of only the best ingredients, she bakes this succulent treat in the early hours of morning, filling our home with alluring scents. Friends are invited to sample the tasty treat. Her son longs for a pie or two when he visits. Of course, it is pure therapy to buffer my pains of aging with feel-good "brown bag apple pie" indulgence.

Any remotely special occasion is reason enough for celebration, not just birthdays, graduations, and holidays, but any day with a hint of gratitude. She collects and stores special gifts for special occasions. All are delicately wrapped with tissue and love in gift bags tied with colorful ribbons. I wonder if this outpouring of gifts will ever cease. No wonder; it won't, it can't because a perfectly happy heart is never empty.

She teaches a vital lesson: a happy heart is an expression of love for the goodness of life itself. It is not what you give, but how it is given that matters most, touching others and speaking to them, of being included in "her heart." When she awakens this morning, I wonder where her heart will take her, what joy she will bring to others today.

My Old Mountaineering Pack

ॐ

Transitioning our home into a bed and breakfast years ago, I was overwhelmed by the need to downsize, disposing of accumulated stuff rapidly. In a storage container in my barn, I came upon my North Face mountaineering backpack. Improvements in outdoor gear over thirty years rendered my old pack obsolete. However, upon opening it, I was delighted to find some of my old gear.

There were stories inside my pack eager to leap out and to be told.

Holding my mountaineering *sunglasses*, I could see ice scratches on the outer leather eye protectors. I found myself instantly transported forty-years back to my first climb up Mt. Hood, hiking up from Timberline in dense cloud cover, the sun breaking through at 8,000 feet. Reaching the summit from the southern route, we walked across to look northwest and were startled by an ominous black wall, a huge thunderstorm, coming directly at us with high winds and flashes of lightning. It was not in the weather forecast! We immediately retreated and began our descent, only to be hit by wind forcefully spraying ice particles and creating a whiteout situation. We dug a snow cave quickly and crawled in, just as the full force of the dark storm hit us, frightening in its roar and fury. Putting my headlamp on, I noticed blood on the snow and realized that my face was completely bloody and swollen. I neglected to pull my balaclava over my face. My eyes had been fortunately protected by my sunglasses; otherwise, my eyes would have swollen shut. Somewhat shaken by this memory, I jarred myself back to the present. I put my sunglasses on again, adjusted them to fit tightly, and paid tribute to their existence.

My *compass* was a military relic with a crosshair sight and steel case. My Uncle Steve had one like it when I was a boy and we went on hikes. I bought mine in a secondhand outdoor equipment store and used it for over thirty years. At times I had to find my way via compass and map, especially when lost or off-trail. In my mountain sojourns, it was common to not know exactly where I was at times, never totally lost of course, but wandering for hours with compass in hand and sun or stars above. My old compass is in my tsunami survival pack now.

My French-made *crampons* invoke unpleasant memories of adjusting them endlessly to fit my boots tightly, only to have them pop loose at the most inopportune times on steep glaciers or crossing rocky outcroppings. New technology today is much better; yet, I never replaced them. I just got used to them and they got used to me. Their scratches are etched on my Danner boots from too many cross-over traverses.

My *ice axe,* a common REI brand, was in my hand on so many high or steep glaciers over the years. Only twice did I have to seriously self-arrest when unroped, flipping once, and once when roped with others to stop our slide/fall. For sentimental reasons, I purchased a wooden handle ice axe made in 1941 in a tiny Swiss village near the Eiger. Twenty-five years earlier, Linda and I hiked in the Bernese Oberland of Switzerland near this village.

Finding my worn nylon *harness* with attached carabiner reminded me that I wore it constantly at high altitudes when frequently roped up as a team or climbing up some rock face or repelling down it. No point ever taking it off. Even slept with it on if camped near an avalanche zone. My old body will never wear a harness again unless I succumb to willful stupidity.

I found a *headlamp* in my pack that I didn't recognize, extremely old. It reminded me of early morning ascents up a mountain. One ascent was up Mt. Jefferson, breaking camp at 4 AM in a dense fog, barely able to see the trail. Another was my ascent under a full moon and star-filled sky at 1 AM up the final 5,000 feet on Mt. Rainier.

My old *altimeter* was a remarkable discovery. It likely prevented me from walking into crevasses, though I will never know such, yet never fail to have absolute faith in its measure of a mountain. It was Swiss-made and very expensive. I always kept it on a nylon cord around my neck along with my small compass, crampon wrench, and avalanche whistle.

An old *water bottle* was found. Obsolete. I had another one just like it that bounced down the 1,800-foot Jefferson Park glacier on the west side of Mt. Jefferson as I traversed across the top of it, on a fixed line because of blue ice conditions. I hesitated long enough to imagine the bottle was me if I wasn't smart and skilled enough to know what I was doing in this situation. I was humbled by my sudden shortness of breath before regaining my focus on reaching the summit.

Near the bottom were my beloved Danner *boots*, worn and weathered, with crampon marks on the toes. Inside was a pair of thick, woolen socks that I got in Nepal. I oiled my boots countless times to restore their thick leather, only to have them fade and dry up into history. I keep them in my car, hoping to wear them up some remote summit, someday, sometime, somehow, somewhere.

I had hoped to find an old *journal* or two, but I didn't. If I had, it most likely would have been unused. Mountaineering is an exhausting experience lasting most of the day. Crawling into my sleeping bag in search of rest and warmth at night, it is doubtful that I ever took time to write a word. My doubts were confirmed. The reality is that these experiences were never in need of a journal to record them; they were inscribed on my skin and bones.

In the end, my old *pack* was donated, too. Its day had come and gone. Before doing so, I loaded it up, swung it onto my back, and hiked up the hill behind my home for a few hours, haunted by the mysticism of mountaineering memories, remembering a few close calls and good balance along sheer vertical exposures, and revering some appreciated grace from the gods. Incredible summits lifted me into grandeur and beauty. Of course, there were nasty storms and a few injuries and hardships along the way. In another lifetime, I would not hesitate to do it all over again. Along with a few fading scars on my face, hands, and legs, those memories are etched in my heart forever.

On the Beach

Life slows at the beach. We move to a different rhythm in the wind and waves, in the sunshine and stars. You cannot see, only sense it in the birds, trees, and clouds, as they reach out to hold you in their embrace. Their dance becomes your dance: free, wild, compellingly joyful, intimate with the natural world around you.

Hug Point on Northern Oregon Coast

On the beach, my pace slows. Wind and sand hold me back if I try to rush. My breathing slows, too. Around me, seagulls become suspended in flight. Joggers seem to shorten their stride. Kites join in, high above me. The surf reaches out, calling me. Nature has a way of adding inertia to my haste, of hugging me when I wish to be free of it. It is a wonderful thing, for it invites reverence and gratitude for this living planet that gives this gift of life.

The crisp scent of ocean air reminds me to leave my phone, camera, radio, shoes, backpack, and hat at home; only shorts, sandals, and a sweatshirt to stay warm. No more! My walk is close to the water, feet in the surf. I close my eyes and listen to the music in the wind. Breathe the fragrance of the pure ocean air deeply. Let the mist caress my body completely. Remove my sandals and feel the sand between my toes. Spread my arms in the strong gusts, and glide away. My heart reminds me of the deeply mystical presence that flourishes here. I become more alive in this exquisite moment, celebrating my fleeting wondrous existence. Even my philosophy slows down, exposing painful realism, casting my doubts to the stars, as I become one with all that is. We truly cherish our precious existence, here at the beach, on the surface of this tiny planet in the vast cosmos, an intimate part of the final mystery flowing in the abyss of our consciousness. Can you feel it, too? It reaches out to us.

Whether the raging storms of winter or easy surf of summer, it matters not to the human spirit. I will never leave. I will stay here forever. Even when I am gone, a part of me will remain. I will walk with you and hold your hand. And we will be together again, on the beach.

Why Me, God?

℧

A simple question,
intriguingly philosophic
with a simple answer
in the beginning,
in the end.

I was taken:
no choice,
no chance,
simply taken
forever.

Smitten with
a blind burst
of passion.
Thought fleeting,
love filling
my entire being.

I barely knew
this woman
engaging me
so completely,

weaving her heart
with mine.

Over five decades
span our journey
together.
I wonder still:
why me,
why was I
so lucky?

REFLECTIONS

Just a Sign

ൟ

A stormy Sunday morning convinces me not to jog in the hard rain. Coffee and a New York Times suffice in a comfortable leather chair at my favorite coffeehouse. Later, as I drive home and stop at a corner, a cardboard sign held by a homeless person or perhaps a less homeless con artist, catches my attention.

PLEASE ANYTHING WILL HELP
HOMELESS AND HUNGRY

Rolling down my window and handing out a dollar, a quick smile and nod of appreciation greet me from a familiar face. Having seen him before, picking bottles out of garbage cans, I have faith that his need is genuine. When I try to empathize with his predicament, however, I cannot imagine trading places. His clothes are dirty and weathered, wet from the rain, and his smile is filled with missing teeth. Yet, he persists in standing in the cold rain and wind. I doubt if I could do that, but in the face of hunger it may be my only choice. While the weather may serve his advantage in provoking sympathy, this thought is quickly dismissed, as I drive on.

Reaching another corner, there is another panhandler, a young woman. She is standing and shivering in the pounding rain under a garbage bag. A big dog lies at her feet, for protection no doubt. Her eyes glare at me, begging for a spark of recognition or guilt. Her sign is more desperate.

NEED TO GET HOME TO CALIFORNIA
MOTHER IS VERY SICK AND NEEDS ME
PLEASE HELP ME PLEASE

I notice her body art and piercings and wonder how she affords such costs. She smokes anxiously. I have seen her before with different signs, of course, on other street corners. Even so, a dollar is offered and appreciation is quickly expressed as she moves on to the next vehicle. We never have eye contact much less a smile, so I feel a bit conned until I consider that desperation generates urgency. A can of food or article of clothing may have been a safer bet, not one that can be used for alcohol or drugs or tattoos. Save that thought for another day with more common sense. Today, the need is starkly in front of me, and I cannot resist the urge to help in spite of my reservations.

After running a few errands, I find myself in another neighborhood with other street corners and more signs, of course. One catches my attention as I slow for a stop.

BROKE & VEGAN
TRYING TO BE HEALTHY
TRYING TO FIND A JOB
HELP IS TRULY APPRECIATED

I roll down my window and hand out a vegan cookie. The man looks at it, somewhat disappointedly. His reaction disquiets me, and I wonder if the "vegan" is merely a con to catch my attention. No matter; at least he has a healthy cookie. I ignore the fact that he is in his twenties, well groomed, wearing nice clothes and shoes, and has money for cigarettes. I wonder if my ignorance serves his greed. Do I wonder too much? If I see him again, I may not roll down my window. I may turn up my radio and speed by.

The storm is worsening, and as I read yet another sign on another street corner, I sense being in the midst of a panhandling epidemic. My ethical high ground is shaky. I drive by and do not offer a dollar. Instead, I pull over, park, and walk back to engage a man with a simple sign with blurred letters, barely readable in the rain.

NEED HELP

COLD AND HUNGRY

He is an older man, like me, perhaps in his sixties, fortunately with a rain jacket, though his pants and shoes are soaked. He is apparently sick with a cold. I speak to him, asking about his need. He explains that he lives under a tarp by the river, or, if he is removed by the police, in any place he can find shelter until he is removed again. I ask him about going to a community shelter, and he explains that they are available only for a few nights. It seems that he could make more money by finding a job. He tells me that he has tried, but few employers would consider him because he cannot read well and lives on the streets. He asks, "Would you hire me?" I struggle with an answer, privately conceding that I would not. Am I mistaken about his reliability? Is it more of a question of acceptability? Is judgment trumping compassion? Fearing the answers, I ask him if I can buy him a hot meal; he appears surprised, quickly agrees, and we walk together to a nearby fast-food vendor. I join him, slowly drinking my coffee, as he eats the burger in two fast bites, and asks if he can have another. I buy him two more. He is truly hungry, and I doubt if it is merely an act for my benefit. He tells me of having been a young man in California, of being married twice and later divorced because of his alcoholism and inability to keep a job. He confesses of only recently "slaying his demons," having been through numerous rehabilitation programs. He leaves to use the bathroom, and I never see him again.

I walk slowly back to my car, pondering what happened. I doubt if he conned me. He seemed to be very needy and even embarrassed, though I endeavored to be sensitive to his predicament. It seems that there has to be community resources available to help him, yet I confess of being totally ignorant of such.

Stopping at a hardware store, I notice a man pushing a grocery cart filled with soda cans. I engage him, asking how it is going. He comments that he is trying his best to survive, asking me if I have any cans. I don't. I commend him for his efforts, as the rain lets up. Bravely, I ask him if collecting cans is better than standing on a street corner with a sign. He points to the sign on his cart.

NO STREET CORNER FOR ME

EARNING MY WAY EACH DAY

WITH THE HELP OF GOD

There is pride in his eyes, though his clothes are worn and his personal hygiene is poor. He further explains that he wants to avoid fights with other homeless persons for the best corners, that it is competitive and nasty at times. He moves on without further comment, waving back at me. A man on a mission. I commit to putting our redeemable cans and bottles in my car, in the event I encounter him again. I privately admire his resolve, imagining that it would be my preferred option if my world collapsed around me.

I drive to the local market, parking to observe yet another presumably homeless person with a sign. Too far away to read the sign, but close enough to observe the passing motorists, most of whom never slow down to offer help. It seems that most of us choose to ignore "beggars." I wonder about the rationalization of those who ignore offering help, keeping their windows closed and music turned up. I suspect that when they see me offering help, they must shake their heads in dismay. I really don't care what they think! They are caged by their stereotypes and prejudices and become the cause of their own eclipse. Fifteen minutes pass and not a single person stops to offer help. There must be a better way to help the homeless and poor. In spite of this thought, I find little resolve in my own being to make a political difference. I am disappointed in myself. I walk away, my philosophy compromised. Life goes on.

Later, driving home, I watch for Jerome. He has been a "regular" on south-side street corners for the past few years. During that time, we have come to know each other by our first names. His sign is simple:

HELP PLEASE

Jerome is fifty-something, wears the same weathered clothes every day, and spends his nights camping at a local park, near a stream for drinking water. A very meager existence: no heat in the cold of winter, little shelter, and just the clothes on his body for warmth and protection. Not having seen him for about a month, I am a bit concerned. I drive around looking for him, hoping to buy him his favorite chicken sandwich at McDonald's. He is surprisingly literate and informed, yet when I inquire into his personal history, he says he dropped out of school at a young age. I endeavor not to inquire too much, for fear that he, too, would disappear. When he sees my wife in her VW Beetle drive up to his corner, he waves and calls her by name. He has become our street corner friend, yet he resists taking too much from us. At last, as the rain lets up, I find him walking down the street, with clean clothes on. I pull over and talk to him, discovering he is in a homeless shelter at a local church and even has a part-time job with a token income. He is no longer on the street corner. I congratulate him, and we hug. He walks away, and I wonder if our paths will ever cross again, but no matter, he is on the upside of life, being lifted by the better angels of our nature and his.

A little research reveals that the homeless are a growing concern in my community. Numbers and needs far surpass resources available for temporary shelter and meals. Having just read an article in our local Sunday newspaper, I am reminded of diminishing federal and state funding of social services, and even less support from charitable agencies with private funding to address such needs. I become despondent, stopping for another cup of coffee and a local newspaper.

Among the needy, of course, are the less needy in search of a handout. Unable to discern the difference, it seems best to err on the side of providing help to a homeless person and forgive our naivete in enabling the drug addict or alcoholic. My moral self-talk tells me that it is simply the right thing to do. After all, I can afford a few dollars each day, though it adds up to fifty dollars each month. My questions fade into more pressing thoughts as I drive on. Yet, a tremor of social injustice vibrates in my being, faint and fleeting mostly, like the mist on my windshield obscuring my sight momentarily, slowing me down before I wipe it unthinkingly away.

I seek higher ground whenever doubts lace my philosophy about street corner ethics. It seems that all societies marginalize their helpless, those who are illiterate and uneducated, physically and mentally disabled, chronically unemployed, caught in the webs of poverty and chronic illness, without the resources to cope. In countries with robust economies, the sharp divide between rich and poor becomes more apparent. This plight is often ignored with sweeping condemnation that such people would not be poor or homeless if they simply made an effort to work hard and manage their lives. There may be truth here, maybe, but the facts suggest otherwise. It seems more ethical to recognize that the helpless and homeless are more often the unfortunate victims of the rest of us who prosper, especially in a free market economy, as competition can be a brutal force on the weak and powerless.

Philosophers remind us that there is no justice in the universe. Life goes on, unrelenting in its pace and complications. Among the homeless on the streets, life may be just barely fair enough to survive, maybe. Consider that this is a human problem that we all need to be committed to address if not solve, in the least, one street corner at a time.

Doppelgänger Effect

ॐ

We like ourselves
prefer others like us
no ugly surprise
this righteous bias

Friends sought
with common views
in art, politics, religion
so much more or less

Convictions shared
forfeit passion
defect ignorance
construct reality

Circles tighten
shut others out
cage others in
a cloistered world

Caring less about
what we miss
utterly irrelevant
benignly blatant

As life confounds
this path forward
we opt to retreat deeper
within our tiny bubble

As strangers touch us
our bubble burst
we opt to reach farther
for a new horizon

We may be more
not less among
others unlike us
in a brave world

Awakenings

ॐ

Sleepless tonight, I arise too early in search of anything that will lead me to a restful state. It seems my mind is spinning in the silent darkness, ignoring the call of my tired physical body. I relax in my old leather chair with a soft light behind me, read from a book in my current stack, listen to gentle "Greek Island" instrumentals, open the window slightly to feel the night wind, and drift away into another philosophical dimension. The literature, music, and night air seem to invigorate me rather than relax me. Philosophy seems to call me. I set the book aside, turn down the music, open the window wider, and begin to think my own thoughts, allowing my mind to take me away. No distractions or predilections.

It seems that life is full of insightful *awakenings*, albeit only when we can fully lay aside distractions. In daily life, we are caught in the patterns of our habits and culture. We attend to "things" and accumulate "stuff." It is both necessary and nonsensical. Human interaction seems mostly superficial, touching only the surface of being with our conversations and exchanges. At day's end, I often sense an existential loss in my search for meaning, for finding heart in my life experiences. Searching for higher ground, I reflect on little things in ordinary life that may have an extraordinary impact. Taking time to pause and tell a person that I admire and appreciate them is not easy in our culture, such gestures appear to be disingenuous. Taking time to listen to those closest to me share their feelings and stories, I feel an emotional link, drawing me into a deeper bond with them. There is profound intimacy surrounding me here, enriching the intensity of emotion and authenticity. The meaningfulness of such exchanges is clear, calling me to rise from the pace of daily living into a new awakening, flowing not from the silent darkness, but a place of abundant light. We transcend our habits and culture, our daily existence, to touch others in a more complete and real manner. The sun is rising on a new day, a more profound opportunity to be and become. Romancing such idealism is healthy.

In midlife, I endeavored to find time to escape alone to hike in high mountains for a few days. During the day, I beheld the beauty and wonder around me—blankets of colorful wildflowers, clear water streams, the wind flowing over nature around me, and the maze of clouds along with a few eagles soaring above me. It felt so good to be alive. At night in my tent, sleep often eluded me. I would arise and lay outside under the star-filled sky, chilled but very alive, as the universe beheld me: an awakening of ultimate consciousness perhaps. Here was transcendence into the fullness of life, recounting life stories and embracing the meaning flowing from them. *Awakenings!* In such exquisite moments, I *found heart*. I would awake as the sky brightened in the early morning, outside in the cold, but very warm and complete and centered. Many others have shared similar experiences, but only after the bond of intimate conversation has been strengthened.

I began to long for *awakenings* in my consciousness and in my life experiences. Learning from the feedback of friends about my "blind spots"—countless failures in connecting with others suspended me on the surface of daily living. At first, it was much easier to defend my dysfunctional patterns than to listen with the intent of personal discovery. Listening more fully until my friends had no more to share, even with repeated invitations of disclosure. It was not unsurprising that such intense exchanges lead to an awakening, however unanticipated. The more profound awakening came in brief exchanges in which I acknowledged some insight flowing from the lives of my friends, often seemingly insignificant.

Philosophers, poets, and prophets have reminded us over the centuries that we do not clearly perceive the reality in which we are intimately intertwined and ultimately grounded. Whether in Plato's placement of us in a cave or St. Paul's admonition to us as seeing through a glass darkly or in the sacred texts across all major religious traditions, a common theme arises into our consciousness, that our sense of reality is limited and our sense of rationality is bounded. Yet there is a lingering hope that this is not an immutable human condition, that we can penetrate reality for we may be the cause of our own eclipse. To discover such may lead one to deep introspection, meditation or prayer in search of *awakenings*. More often, it comes from human interaction which reaches beyond superfluity into the realm of intimate personal disclosure and compassion. Even when we lack religious faith, our inner philosophical sense reigns in fueling awakenings, such as those shared by friends, as cited below.

Perceptions are often incomplete and inaccurate. They need to be checked often!

You have blind spots: Some people see you differently than you see yourself.

Asking for helpful feedback is a good thing to do often. Ask for examples.

Emotional reactions may be disproportionate with triggering events. Why?

Active listening is an art form, requiring interaction. Acknowledge feelings!

Empathy is the key to intimacy. Seek to understand before being understood.

Laughter is the key to emotional health. Search for comic relief in nonsense.

No worries. No rush. Take a deep breath and focus on the present!

Take care of yourself first and foremost. Strengthen emotional intelligence (EQ).

Be honest in all affairs. Preserve moral and intellectual integrity.

Life is good, but not fair. Bad things happen to good people. Pick yourself up!

Lots of material stuff causes emotional constipation. Lighten your pack!

Ice cream is the food of the gods. Try a butterscotch milkshake.

The natural world is our real home. Seek adventure in it often.

Good friends are our joy and sorrow. Nurture relationships.

Nothing is certain. Impermanence prevails. Buddha is right!

Change is inevitable. Change is necessary. Change is insightful.

Sharing your heart is a good thing. Invite others to share their hearts, too.

Have a garden. Love flowers and plants. Bring nature into your home!

Dark weather invites dark dispositions—get over it! Go find the sun!

Too much TV is too much TV. Too much golf is too much golf!

Love an animal. Have a pet!

Giving is better than getting. Find something to give away today.

There is undiscovered light in the darkness. Look for it rather than avoid it.

Personal influence is better than positional power.

Little differences add up. Make a difference!

You can be an asshole and not know it. Fix it!

Tell your stories. Even tell them again to yourself in the quiet of night.

Live a life that matters first and foremost!

You become your dreams.

We, You and Me

ও

You are who you are,

I am who I am.

You may not fully

know who I am.

I may not fully

know who you are.

You may not fully

know who you are.

I may not fully

know who I am.

We come together,

remain apart.

I seek to understand

who you are.

You seek to understand

who I am.

Virtues sustain us,

love redeems us.

We engage
not always well,
Mostly converse
maybe listen.
You seek to change
how I think, feel.
I seek to change
how you feel, think.

Weary,
we look away
from whom we are,
remain together.
We may survive,
we may grow.
We may only be
just you and me.

Feedback, the Art Of

ॐ

Feedback sought
opens a window wide
into what we fail
to see, hear, say, feel
enlightening us

Feedback solicited
descriptive, specific
timely, direct
purposefully helpful
enhances awareness

Feedback resisted
general, prescriptive
evaluative, void of examples
maliciously manipulative
shuts us down

Feedback as conversation
never lectured
patiently persistent
listening, reflecting
lifts us up

Feedback inclusive
of self-disclosure
an intimate partner
sharing inner thoughts
ignored feelings

Feedback reveals blindspots
disclosure reveals passion, pain
all fresh air, fortifying trust
opening our window wider
nurturing authenticity

We awaken, arise, learn
seek what we don't see
hear what we don't hear
change what holds us down
be better, become more

Getting to It

ॐ

When was the last time you sat down across from someone who mattered to you and expressed how you felt about them? Across from someone means eye-to-eye and knee-to-knee with no distractions or preoccupations. It is a simple gesture, yet an uncommon, even uncomfortable one in our culture. Too often, we are locked in social patterns which emotionally distance us from each other.

If you were to consider such a prospect, what would you say? You may speak in general terms using evaluative language, rather than describing specific observed behaviors which affect you positively or negatively. "You are a wonderful person" is music to our ears, but of infinitely greater value is "You went out of your way to help me on several occasions by doing ..." "I really appreciated what you did for me." The former is "feel-good" rhetoric, whereas the latter is clearly more helpful. Its specificity is revealing what a person actually did, thus reinforcing its value and repetition. "You are a wonderful person" becomes more meaningful as a capstone emotional embrace after initial specific comments are shared. Otherwise, such a general comment without specificity may seem disingenuous or manipulative.

Years ago, in a leadership development program, we submersed participants in a radically unique process, one without the structure of goals, roles and norms, in which the only directive was to "learn about leadership." The resulting behavioral vacuum led participants to fill it in various ways. Eventually, participants recognized that each other's behavior was an opportunity for learning. Each sharpened their skills in describing what was effective and ineffective, and why. Most people began to see themselves anew. Our conversations became more authentic, intimate, and meaningful. Relationships became more direct and trustful. Social risk-taking was more comfortable. Metaphorically, our "inner window" was opening widely to let fresh air (insights) in.

In these leadership development programs, incredible experiential learning occurred because invited feedback led to insight, insights led to personal self-disclosures, and such disclosures led to further insights and feedback. An incubator of self-discovery and growth! People clearly saw themselves and others, often for the first time. Certainly, not all feedback was accurate or accepted, nor was all disclosure accurate or affirmed. The process, however, departed from common social norms governing social interactions. No longer were we strangers to each other and to ourselves. As social risk was assumed and mutual trust was developed, people began discovering their "blind spots" and revealing their "private self." In a relatively short period of time, they became increasingly functional and healthy in relating to others.

The spouses of program participants would later comment: "What did you do to cause him to share feelings so openly?" "For the first time, we had a real conversation in which we shared how we felt about each other." "She actually listened to me, acknowledged my feelings, and asked for feedback." We were given undeserving credit, for the real catalyst was each person immersed in the process of self-discovery and renewal. Admittedly, the process worked better for some than others at different times in different ways; it was not without social risk and pain.

Yet the effort was professionally guided solely for the benefit of the individual. People came to understand the essence of influence, that effective leaders (and others) rely primarily upon personal relations and influence, not positional power or authority.

So, *getting to it* entails developing strong, functional relationships with people. We don't need to participate in such a program to capture most of its benefits. The poet William Stafford's words echo clearly as we pause to reflect on this challenge:

"If you don't know the kind of person I am,
And I don't know the kind of person you are,
A pattern that others made may prevail in the world,
And following the wrong god home, we may miss our star."

Patterns in our culture cause us to move past each other in a polite, superficial fashion, nearly strangers to each other, fearing intimacy, clinging to mistrust, ignoring the things that matter most, and often giving in to the things that matter least. We have the personal power to disrupt these patterns. We have the capacity to examine our lives and discover "the right gods." Just what is our "star?" I opt to resist a response in favor of allowing you to grapple with that question. My best answer may not be your best answer! Just maybe, we won't know our "star" until we fully embrace life, this adventure of *finding heart*. Get to it! Why not!

Note: This essay is a tribute to the Oregon Leadership Institute over its forty-year history.

Nasty *"d"* Words

A flawed species
human beings
emotions always at play
"*d*" tendencies abound
in the shadows of life
invading our world
taking us captive
caged in *distortion*.

Are you aware of distortion?

A painful migraine
something is wrong
inner conflict
generates *dissonance*
external realities
confront internal beliefs
a miserable space as
facts interfere with truth.

Can you tell when a belief is false?

A supposed friend
tells vital lies about

what we want to believe

invites *denial*

shrinks reality

confounds biases

pretense prevails

authenticity fades.

Can you change a false belief?

An alluring seductress

relentless in pursuit

offers fantasied pleasure

fosters *deception*

believing whatever we want

invites betrayal of heart

actions unchallenged

we live vital lies.

Can you tell when you are living a lie?

A home invading criminal

steals inner reality

holds sanity hostage

inflicts *delusion*

imposes darkness

reconfigures being

cognition fades

contact is lost.

Are you out of touch with reality?

An appealing authority
radicalizes our mind
dispenses disinformation
advocates *dogmatism*
ideologically extreme
basking in superiority
right is might
much better than others.

Do you succumb to fanaticism?

Strata of **"*d*"** tendencies
mostly self-inflicted
bring fear, anger, hate, rage
compounds *dysfunctionality*
integrity compromised
virtue forgotten
new worlds constructed
we alone imagine.

Do you know yourself fully?

A deeper voice
screams at us
something is wrong
inflicts *depression*

wandering the abyss

we reach higher

light finally found

reclaiming ourselves.

Note: we all have **"*d*"** tendencies at different times in different ways for different reasons. One of our most profound qualities is that we can become aware of them, with the power to confront and overcome them, building greater self-respect and authenticity.

Social Philosophy

ॐ

Finding heart is ultimately philosophical, a search for meaning in life experiences. Our social philosophy facilitates or interferes with this search, opening us up (or not) to what truly matters most to us in life.

Social philosophy is essential in "finding heart!"

When was the last time you witnessed an ugly exchange between two people, reflecting irrational malice? A boss saying, "If you don't get your ass in gear, I will kick it out of here." A teacher scolding, "If you would have paid attention once in a while, you might have done better." A family member yelling, "How can you be so stupid or cruel?" A friend crying, "I can't trust anything you say or do." Or, a minister saying, "You need to repent and confess your sins to God."

The reaction is often emotionally excessive, causing us to wonder about what else is going on.

What else is going on?

It may be a matter of *social philosophy,* a deeper social phenomenon, powerful and pervasive, right in front of us, but less transparent in our cognitive milieu. Too often, we mistakenly attribute emotional outrage to personality dysfunctions, character flaws, EQ deficiencies or simply "having a bad day." Social philosophy can be a challenging idea to wrap our minds around. In its simplest form, it entails *a set of implicit assumptions about people.* Such assumptions become the catalyst in activating the "Pygmalion Effect" or self-fulfilling prophesy in which assumptions influence actions, influence reactions, and reactions validate assumptions. A circular web of expectations.

Social philosophy is always at play!

In Greek mythology, Pygmalion carved a beautiful woman (Galatea) out of a block of ivory, fell in love with his creation, and the power of his love caused the woman to become real (with a little help from Venus). Similarly, if we assume people are untrustworthy, we understandably treat them with suspicion and control. When they react with contempt and resistance, it is no great surprise that our initial beliefs are confirmed. However, even if our self-awareness acknowledges this tendency, we are largely oblivious to it.

Why? It is reality! It is simply the way things are!

We construct our own unique *social reality*, based upon our assumptions about people, activated by the pervasive power of the Pygmalion effect. Of course, there are more details between the lines of this simple concept that confound our sense of reality: bounded cognition and rationality, selective perception and observation, causal attribution bias, and dispositional and judgment biases. Unwittingly, we create our own disinformation in affirming our social reality, albeit distorted but nevertheless feeling so very real. We become the cause of our own eclipse.

Social reality does not exist independently. It is constructed!

To be more precise, social philosophy entails a popularized set of positive (progressive) and negative (regressive) assumptions about human nature, disposition, motivation, performance, change, and the human condition. As an example of progressive social philosophy, assumptions about human nature assert most people are responsible, trustworthy, ambitious, capable, and resourceful. Assumptions about human motivation and performance assert most people are honest, can be trusted, capable of autonomous and independent effort, influenced by helpful feedback, and mostly goal driven. Assumptions about human change assert most people are capable and willing to make personal change, not resistant to such, and receptive to external intervention. Assumptions about the human condition focus on a universe in which people alone are responsible for their fates or destiny, external (divine) intervention is unpredictable, and the human condition reflects impermanence and injustice. Given these assumptions, it is relatively easy to conversely develop the negative ones. These assumptions are implicit, powerful, pervasive, ubiquitous, and omnipresent in our lives.

We all have a social philosophy, whether we are unaware of it or not!

The Greek philosopher, Heraclitus, asserted that "change is the only constant." One may wonder: Can a person change their social philosophy? Not easily. It takes time and effort, but most importantly, the will to change. As we think about our social philosophy, we need to "take out the garbage, smelling up the house." Consider that social philosophies may become differentiated based on gender, ethnicity, disability, age, education, socioeconomic status, and religious/political/sexual orientations. A discrimination bias is likely to be at play, including stereotypes and doppelgänger effects. Preferences in affirming assumptions can be unknowingly influenced by family and social development, work, education, media, religion, politics, and economics.

Changing social philosophy requires introspection and feedback!

There is a "best" type of social philosophy: *progressive* because it leads to stronger, healthier, more positive personal and strategic outcomes. One of my first requests to my university students and newly promoted managers is to describe the person for whom they performed their best work. Use one-word descriptors such as "kind" or "tough" or "trusting" or "empowering" or "forceful." The "person" can be a boss, teacher, friend, minister, or coach. No surprise! Most descriptive terms are congruent with a progressive social philosophy. No need to cite a long history of social research which unequivocally supports the same finding. Your social philosophy matters!

Note: For a more exhaustive treatise of social philosophy (and related topics of strategy and culture), see the author's academic book *Reinventing HRM and OD*, UO Press (2016).

Oregon Flood

ॐ

Driving to Portland on a dark winter night, it seemed the rain, wind, and fog pressed in upon me, even pursued me. Several vehicles had hydroplaned off the highway. It was obvious that my windshield wipers were overdue for replacement. Immersed in the riptide of spray from trucks, passing them was a blind leap of faith, perhaps an act of willful stupidity. Concentration was indeed exhausting. Heavy rains continued their constant assault all day and night for most of the week. Clouds were low, black, and foreboding. No birds filled the skies, no squirrels romped in trees, no lovers sat on park benches, and no kids played on playgrounds. No sunrises or sunsets either. Just more rain creating soaked lawns, overfilled drains, and flooded basements. Rivers were steadily rising, not just from the record rainfall, but from snowmelt in the mountains due to warming temperatures. Low-lying areas began to flood. Otherwise complacent people started to panic.

It seemed like the winter of 1996 would never end. Unlike regions to the east, western Oregon doesn't turn into a bitter cold, snow packed landscape in winter. It stays relatively moderate, and rains and rains and rains. Complaining about too much rain and praying for sunshine are persistent cultural rites. Seasonal affective disorder (SAD) is a very transparent community health problem.

Working in my east Portland office, listening to the emergency radio band, it was clear that the city was in peril. If the river breached the seawall, the downtown core would be overcome by a huge, fast-flowing river, carrying destroyed property and other debris from low-lying areas. To my surprise, most people were indifferent to the civic call for volunteers. Their homes were on high ground and not in danger, and besides, they had jobs to do. Surely, others in the community could step up: maybe the homeless, welfare recipients, college students or unemployed. Somebody else! It's just not "my problem." Staring at my computer screen, responding to emails, the river seemed far away; besides, my home was on high ground in Eugene (120 miles south). As I thought about the situation, an inner voice began to call me, only a faint whisper at first, deep inside, speaking to me, again and again. A voice reminding me that if we have the skill and energy, we must help, must sacrifice, not tomorrow but today. It continued to speak to me, refusing to be silenced, too strong to ignore, a familiar haunting voice. I recognized it, sensed its urgency, shut off my computer, and hurried out of my office. There was little doubt about where I needed to be, where I wanted to be, where I had to be.

Floods were historically common in western Oregon, particularly in river basins joining the Willamette and Columbia Rivers. Many farms and towns had been built in floodplains. No need to fear! After all, the last major flood was in 1964, and a massive system of flood control had been constructed since then. But constant heavy rain creates existential angst, trumping even our most confident intelligibility. People began to sense that the winter of 1996 was peculiarly ominous. Rivers were already above record levels, and meteorological forecasts predicted no change in weather patterns. The Portland community was alarmed when it was predicted the Willamette River would rise and flow over the concrete seawall that protects the downtown core, likely requiring a major evacuation of citizens and causing hundreds of millions of dollars in property damage. The mayor pleaded for volunteers with carpentry skills to assist in building a barrier, reinforced with sandbags, above the sea wall. A community drama was about to unfold. A drama that would fuel my passion.

I returned to my apartment, changed my clothes, grabbed a few tools, and headed to the downtown riverfront. Crossing the river, I realized it had widened twofold, and it had risen to within twelve feet of cresting the seawall. I imagined being swept away by the current, struggling to survive in the frigid water, and succumbing to it. Too much danger and too few rescue resources! It was absolutely frightening! Even overpowering and omniscient! I was quickly assigned to one of the construction teams working along the river, erecting the plywood barriers above the seawall, cutting, drilling, and bolting them in place. The rain never stopped nor did we. The prospect of our meager efforts fending off the might of nature was dauntless. There was persistent skepticism that we could build a sufficiently strong barrier to hold back the river in the short time left. We endeavored to silence that dark voice! Our team had an amazing synergy like bees in a hive pulsing with a rhythm in cadence with the wind and rain. Other crews filled and placed sandbags against our barriers. By late afternoon, the barriers were complete.

Surprised by indifference among citizens to volunteer, I was seriously annoyed when it translated into curiosity. People began to crowd on the bridges safely above us, umbrellas in hand, to watch our efforts. I wondered if they privately hoped for the worst, finding entertainment in tragedy. Schadenfreude! They contributed to traffic jams that hindered our efforts in delivering supplies. We mostly ignored them, though I fantasized having a long hook to pull them over the railing into our ranks, and confess of shouting at them once to come down and join us, that we needed more help.

Once the barriers were in place, some crews moved to the east side of the river. I stayed behind to work with a sandbag crew. We worked in a seemingly disjointed frenzy at first. I was handed a shovel when a new truckload arrived with bags and sand. Dumped at our feet, once again a magical rhythm emerged in our work crew. Two of us filled bags held by two nurse volunteers, and two local bank employees stacked the bags for delivery. Hundreds upon hundreds of bags were filled. Each new load was attacked with a compulsive purposeful vigor; bodies in lines, bags moving like factory assemblies. We labored together for nearly four hours of sweat, sore muscles, laughter, and good spirit, with an unspoken commitment to our community. Finally, our tasks were complete; barriers were in place, as the river continued to rise. We hoped for the best and were later rewarded for our efforts.

Exhausted, cold and soaked, my constant motion kept me warm during my ten-hour sojourn. In the late evening, I was released to go home, pledging to return if needed the next morning. I jogged the three miles home to stay warm and found a hot bath waiting for me, along with tea and a kiss. This day could have passed as another workday, with decisions and tasks that would inevitably fade into insignificance. Instead, the things I did with the people I did them with are deeply etched into my heart forever. The voice within me was silent, but I could sense my father's smile, knowing his teachings will be his gift to me forever.

We Knew

෬

I knew. I want my grandchildren and their children to know that I shamefully knew. The quality of your environment is less because of my generation. I was able to do little to avert this trend.

Public action regarding environmental concerns has been trumped by economic, political, and religious issues and interests. No great surprise that humanity is incapable of apprehending future risks of survival if it requires sacrificing immediate pleasures. We have our collective heads in the sand of short-term self-interests.

Our best science clearly tells us that we are on the verge of crossing a threshold of irreversible environmental decline and degradation. The basic argument is sound: environmental degradation threatens human survival; human survival is of great value; therefore, we have a moral obligation to avert such degradation. This argument is imminently sound, overwhelmingly empirically evidenced and logically supported.

Sound arguments are seldom persuasive in the face of strongly opposing interests. The most common countervailing argument is: environmental degradation is overstated, based on bad science (BS); economic prosperity and standard of life are of high value and outweigh such concerns; therefore, we have an obligation to better the immediate conditions of life for all. A politically more appealing and persuasive argument, but with less empirical evidence and riddled with logical fallacies. Moreover, we are willfully stupid enough to believe that our science will rescue us, inventing new technologies to reverse environmental declines and to restore the health of our planet. Ignorant imagination trumps intelligence, again.

I envision environmental nightmares: rising temperatures and sea levels, air and water pollution, resource depletion, new diseases, crop failures, declines in biodiversity, etc. The collective impact is a planet at peril, thus humanity at peril. I suspect my grandchildren will scorn us, me. What were you thinking, Grandpa? How could you be so irresponsible? You are right, of course. I deserve your moral indictment. Our entire generation does. Our gift to you is a pending apocalypse. Shame on us.

Your grandmother and I just listened to Kathleen Dean Moore talk about her new book, *Moral Ground*, at the University of Oregon tonight. We will do what we can in our lives to treat our planet well, knowing that our political systems are so dysfunctional and corrupt that global action to avert an environmental crisis is unlikely. The ghosts of Edward Abbey and Rachael Carson haunt me. We will hold their torches high to push back the darkness around us.

Sadness wraps around my being like an iron blanket. I am sad that I could not leave this planet, much less our society, in a better condition than when I arrived. Let this contrition be a call to action for you and your children: Do the greatest good for the most people you can—protect our planet!

Outback

ભ

Heading to an outback town in a western state, I was charged with "fixing" employee unrest at a small sawmill. Initial reports were that more than thirty employees wanted to unionize, but their reasons were unclear. For my company, a large paper and wood products corporation with mostly unionized operations, the prospect of a small operation unionizing was not an issue, as nonunion employees already received the same wages and benefits. Rather, the issue was the employee unrest itself which included threats of a wildcat strike, resulting in a cessation of operations.

When I arrived, a shift change was in progress. Departing employees looked at me with suspicion, avoiding contact even though I greeted them in a friendly manner. The mill was small and weathered in appearance, with a few old mobile home trailers near it, one of which was the manager's office.

The manager's office had a huge desk, a few chairs and filing cabinets, piles of clutter, and behind the desk was a large window with an equally large aquarium. In it was the largest rattlesnake I had ever seen. Departing employees had to leave the mill by walking past this window to get to the parking area. As they walked by, the manager picked up a mouse, wrote the name of an employee on its belly with a bright colored marker, then held the mouse over the tank to feed the snake, holding it long enough for all employees to see. As the employee whose name was on the mouse's belly walked by, the manager would bang on the window and laugh. He turned to explain that when an employee failed to cooperate or perform his job, he was a "targeted man" and now he knew it, that he "could run, but couldn't hide" as he would be fired shortly. I was in shock. This practice was appalling.

I left the office to walk around the mill and talk directly to employees. The manager intended to accompany me, but I insisted that he not do so. I presented a letter to him from his superior, stating my complete authority to resolve the situation, including terminating his employment. Telling employees that I was from the regional HR office, that I was here to listen to complaints, and that conversations would be confidential, seemed to relax them. It was clear that they disliked the manager and his practices and only had faith in Harold, their informal advocate. I sought out Harold, explained my mission, and we took a long walk together. My worst nightmares were confirmed.

I presented the manager with a list of employee complaints, and he confessed that he was aware of them, but they interfered with his authority. He asked if I intended to "fire" him. My response was affirmative if he refused to change. He informed me that he was quitting and was vacating the premises immediately; I even helped him load his aquarium (and rattlesnake) in his pickup truck. I advised my superiors of his actions, and that I wanted to find a local replacement if possible; they agreed.

After he left, I announced over the mill intercom that he was gone, and a loud cheer arose among the employees. Stating the minimal qualifications, I asked for any interested persons to come to the office for an interview; only two persons arrived, but not Harold. That puzzled me, so after the interviews, I sought out Harold and asked him to apply; he was reluctant. Yet, he was clearly the best-qualified person to do the job with both experience and a college education … and the respect of employees. Toward the end of the day, I offered the manager job to Harold. His response was intriguing: "Come to my home for dinner and lodging, to meet my family, and if you still want to offer the job to me in the morning, I will accept it." I agreed.

After we shut down the mill and secured the premises, Harold and I drove about forty-five minutes to his home along windy back roads, deeper into the countryside. Our conversation mostly focused on the mill operation. Finally, at the top of a hill on a gravel road, I saw a small valley below me with a beautiful village and well-groomed fields. The village had a school, store, fire station, and town hall. All of the homes were well maintained and fairly large. We entered Harold's log home, and he asked me to sit in the entryway while he gathered his family. To my surprise, I noticed a Book of Mormon on a side table. Harold indicated that they were Mormons, but not affiliated with the Salt Lake church. He then introduced me to his three wives and told me that they practiced polygamy. While I had been aware of Mormon sects, I was a bit stunned to be actually in the midst of one. A deep breath and a big smile! The children would appear later. Harold seemed to study me closely, as I did him. Yet, there was an easy bond between us.

We had dinner at a huge table, complete with prayer and song. The children were well mannered, though gleeful and relaxed. After dinner, Harold and I walked around the village, as their lifestyle and religious customs were explained to me. I noticed that people referred to Harold as Bishop. There was nothing that I observed that alarmed me. To the contrary, it was a very peaceful community, even with music and dance later at the town hall. After joining them for family prayer, I retired for the evening and arose to an early breakfast. Driving back to the mill, I asked Harold to accept the job, and he did. And he held the position for nearly a decade until the mill closed.

My experience there was one that I have always cherished. There was never much reservation in me to embrace Harold as a good man. In no way would I permit religious prejudice or intolerance to cloud my views, even if societal laws deemed such practices as illegal. Over forty years have passed, and I occasionally wonder about Harold and his community. I trust that his faith has sustained him, and my faith wishes him well.

Note: I have been guarded to share this experience for fear that this community would be threatened. Time has hopefully dissipated such concerns.

Zen and the Art of Carpentry

ೞ

Philosophers have found mysticism arising out of motorcycle maintenance, fly fishing, ballet, mountaineering, flower gardening, sailing, music composition, to name a few. I opt for carpentry, learned at the feet of my father and grandfather.

The art of carpentry seems to have more in common with sculpture than with other crafts. It entails vision translated into planning, the use of hand tools and natural materials, precise measurement, considerable physical work, and enduring vision. It is an act of creation in which some "work of art" is produced such as furniture or architecture. The skills of the artist reach beyond the mere use of tools and materials, to imagination and contemplation. Deep concentration and disciplined detachment are found when the artist is caught up in the creative process. Time is without conscious apprehension as one gives in to flow of consciousness with a highly concentrated focus.

There is a mystic dimension to carpentry. It is grounded in the physical manipulation of natural materials to bring something new into existence. Because carpentry requires the intricate interplay of form and function, the artist becomes inseparable from the artwork. The creative process produces a mindfulness focused solely on the art. Just as pieces of a jigsaw puzzle come together to form more than the sum of its parts, so does the artwork of the carpenter.

With deeper immersion, a higher state of consciousness is attained, a place of solitude and inner vision. In this state, the artwork flows from the immediate euphoric embrace of the creative process to the aesthetic empowerment arising out of the artist. In that embrace, there is a heightened sense of connectivity with all that is, all that exists, and the underlying cosmic reality which produces and sustains it. The creations of the carpenter become a new part of reality, expanding the reach of being, touching something beyond the ordinary and orthodox.

The Big Yellow House

When I built my home, tools and material in hand, I was lifted by every piece of lumber I cut and every nail I pounded to a new place in relation to the natural world around me. After sustained effort, I would pause and my heart would sing. It percolated a reverence for living things, for the former living things that became part of my home, as they now surrounded me in their embrace. Is it any wonder that I revered my home? Is it any wonder that it has enriched my sense of place? It came from the earth just as I. My carpentry takes me to a place in which the mystic in me rejoices because of what it truly teaches me.

In the end, carpentry is art. Art invokes mysticism. In mysticism of my craft, I *find heart*.

Philosophy of Life

ॐ

(notes to my grandchildren)

It is so easy to float along on life's journey and never pause to reflect upon the things that matter most in seeking or creating experiences that touch and nourish our being. The list below is some advice to my grandchildren, in the hope that they will listen to my voice, albeit remote, and ponder my words.

1. *Believe in yourself!* Be your own best friend, not your own worst enemy. Your promise and potential are extraordinary and will be primarily enhanced by your willingness to have faith in who you are and can become.

2. *Take care of yourself!* Continue to strengthen your emotional intelligence and health, and your physical health and fitness throughout your life. If you do, you will enjoy your life journey more fully. Besides, where else will you live?

3. *Take time to think deeply!* Find time alone to read and philosophically reflect on what matters most to you. Adopt a questioning attitude and be willing to critically examine the "known" throughout your life. Doubt is a good thing! However, approach the "unknown" with a sense of wonder and reverence, not fear.

4. *Find space to feel deeply!* Share your feelings, acknowledging and honoring them. Allow emotional engagement and immersion in the wonders of life. Embrace causes that add meaning and uplift the human condition.

5. *Enjoy play and adventure!* Allow a part of you to never grow up. While work is essential in accomplishing goals, too much work is too much work. Take time to play, and most importantly, to be playful. Seek new life adventures.

6. *Trust fully!* Trust others and honor their trust. Look out for the interests of others in their absence. Seek lasting friendships based on trust and respect. Trust may be violated, but don't avoid friendship simply to protect yourself.

7. *Love fully.* Affirm that love matters most in life. Offer it wisely, and forgive others and yourself if you fail. Dream about affirming love, as it will enhance your capacity to love, even to love yourself fully.

8. *Embrace reverence for all life!* Let reverence fill every fiber of your being. Cherish and protect all living things. Life matters. Your life matters! Protect the earth. Be environmentally engaged.

9. *Rejoice in small wonders!* There are so many little things that brighten the immense darkness and chaos around us. Look for them, hold them up high, and let them speak to you and teach you.

10. *Work purposefully!* It is essential to not only work hard and long but for a specific purpose; otherwise, you will lose motivation and energy. Fight for a better future. Be politically engaged.

11. *Enjoy your greater family!* Plan time to see your cousins and do 'fun' things with them. You will be a source of strength and compassion to each other. Friends will come and go, but your cousins will always be family.

As you reflect on this list, you will discover important things that I failed to mention. That warms your grandfather's heart, as you are thinking philosophically. Indeed, I would encourage you to develop your own list, to fully clarify and affirm your *philosophy of life*. Review it often and endeavor to affirm it throughout your life.

The Monk and the Trekker

ॐ

It was my first full day in Nepal. I was intent on discovering the temples and bazaars of Katmandu, to wander far and get as lost as possible, and to find surprise around every corner and in every garden park. I wanted to talk to the locals, endeavoring to learn the basics of their language, and to avoid tourists, especially Americans. It was easy to get lost in the ancient labyrinth of endless streets and alleys, but overwhelming to absorb the culture, with all of its color, art, traditions, smells, sounds, people, and crafts. Of major interest were artifacts of their cultural history.

Resting from hours of walking, I found myself in the square of a holy Buddhist temple, surrounded by beautiful school children who were playing and singing songs. One little boy approached me, saying: "Do you speak English?"

"Yes, I do. I am American."

The boy giggled and waved for more children to join us. Soon, I was engulfed by more than twenty children, beautiful faces, big dark eyes, bright smiles, and boundless energy. They were saying: "Good day."

I responded "Namaste." I took a few photos before their teacher herded them away down a narrow alley back to school. Their laughter echoed in the distance, warming my heart. Even in this amazingly poor country in an incredibly harsh environment, children are indeed bright lights of joy.

As I rose to move on, a Buddhist monk walked toward me, greeting me with "Namaste," and to my surprise, spoke flawless English, asking: "You are here for the mountains?"

"Yes, I am. I plan to fly to Pokhara tomorrow, and hike for three weeks into the Annapurnas."

He smiled for an instant, then sat down and crossed his legs, asking if we could converse. I agreed, imagining he was a reincarnated Mormon missionary ready to provide me with the Buddhist equivalent of the Book of Mormon, the Tripitaka, Mahayana, or Tibetan Book of the Dead. Relief! He had nothing in his possession.

"So, why do you go to the mountains?" He inquired.

"I go to embrace their grandeur and beauty."

"And you plan to climb them?" He asked with a serious look.

"I plan to climb some very high ridges but mostly trek around them and over their passes. I plan to enjoy the Rhododendron forests, too; the entire natural environment."

"What do you seek?"

I sensed a purpose underlying his curiosity. Yet, I was intrigued and willing to tolerate his intrusion. "I seek incredible scenery, fresh air, and the wonder of nature. I seek to learn from the Nepali about their culture and traditions, too."

He listened closely and smiled. "Yes, you will find these things, but what do you seek beyond those? Is there something deeper that you want for yourself?" I thought that I was on the verge of a religious promotion, but I sought no escape route. I was indeed curious about his perspective and what I might learn, so I continued the conversation.

"If you're suggesting God or nirvana, I don't expect to find those things. I have no higher metaphysical purpose, though I am open to discovery. Further, I don't practice meditation either. I am just a dumb American." Comic relief!

He laughed and said: "I'm not trying to convert you to Buddhism. I just enjoy philosophical discussion." Music to my ears: philosophy.

The monk inquired further, "So, what do you truly seek in going into the mountains? Is there something deeper in yourself?" Do I really want to get into this discussion in the first place, I wondered. Oh hell, why not for a little while? Maybe I will learn more about the Nepali culture.

"I suppose I seek peace of mind, a sense of well-being connected with the natural environment, a sense of wholeness and wonder. Maybe even a mystical experience or two."

"And you believe you will find this state of being in the mountains?" I sensed where this conversation was headed. So, I thought I would engage in some direct philosophical engagement; after all, this was a monk sitting across from me, orange robe and sandals, immersed in Buddhism.

"Maybe, but I could get lost in the mountains. But getting lost doesn't worry me, as I can still find what I am seeking even if I am lost."

The monk smiled and said: "You are a philosopher."

"Just an old skeptic with lots of questions and fewer answers. A seeker first and foremost."

"You are a humble man. That is a very good virtue. Since you like questions, may I ask you another?"

"Sure." I thought the monk was going to provide me with a teaching moment.

"Do you think you can only find what you seek in the mountains? Perhaps, you can find it right here where we are sitting?" He was clearly self-confident and challenging me.

"I seriously doubt that I can find here what I would find in the mountains. I don't see high snowcapped summits or beautiful vistas."

"What about the peace of mind and the well-being you seek?" The monk asked, inching toward me slightly, his arms open to me.

"I think there are too many distractions here, too much noise and movement. Ok, I sense you are suggesting I could, probably through meditation; right?"

"Yes, of course. And if that is possible, why climb the mountain in the first place?"

"Because I don't really know if what I can find there is the same thing that I might find here? Such an assumption might lead to false equivalency. Unless I experience the mountains intimately, I might never know."

"You are a good thinker. But if you embrace the same sense of well-being here, you can avoid the dangers of mountain climbing?"

"Theoretically, I suppose so. But why not do both? There is the pure enjoyment of the mountaineering experience that I would not have here? I prefer hiking to meditating any day of the week. Plus, the sheer exertion and risk might make me more susceptible to mystical experiences. But let me ask you a question?"

"Of course, I love questions."

"We share that in common! My question is why you chose to be a monk?"

"To seek enlightenment." His response was quick, ringing of absolute truth.

"And certainly, there are monasteries in the mountains where you can practice meditation? Isn't that why those places were built? And in those places, there may be greater opportunities for peace and serenity, even for enlightenment."

"Yes, of course."

"So even though you may not climb mountains, you enjoy being high in them because of the environment it provides? And you would never know that if you don't go there? And never know, I might add, if what you experience is substantively different than what you experience here?"

"You argue your point well."

"So, if you can attain the same depth of enlightenment through meditation by sitting here, why build monasteries? I suspect that there is an important reason! It seems that we are not too different in going to high places for the difference it creates from where we are now?"

"I see your point. There are different advantages to both." Smiling. "But if you think that these mystical experiences can only occur in the mountains, you may be missing an opportunity to encounter them right here; don't you think?"

"Yes, of course. It is difficult for me, given the distractions in this place, even sitting in the shadow of your temple, even with the soothing sound of temple chimes, to create a quiet place within myself. Ear plugs and a face mask might help."

The monk laughed. "You have a sense of humor, too. That is a very good thing! May I ask another question?"

"Sure. You ask one, and then I will. I still want to understand what the enlightenment is you seek and how you recognize it when attained?" I sensed he was eager to respond.

"What do you know about Buddhism?" He asked.

"Not much," I replied. "I recall emphasis on enlightenment and achieving nirvana. Belief in three or four truths, too. I don't think you believe in God, and your afterlife entails reincarnation, but I am unsure. A Buddhist friend once told me that it was about first recognizing the things that positively affect your being, second avoiding the things that negatively impact it, and third developing the ability to embrace the positive and abandon the negative. Something like that."

"That is an interesting way of putting it. I like it. I would add that recognition of positives and negatives requires much reflection, but the task of developing one's self may take many lifetimes. Of course, there is much more to it."

"I get to ask my question. Can you help me to understand the concept of enlightenment?"

The monk smiled. "My favorite topic."

Before he could respond, however, I heard bells in the distance, and the monk rose quickly, indicating that he had to return to the temple. He asked if I could meet him again tomorrow, but I could not. I stood and thanked him for his time. He bowed and said, "Namaste." I did the same.

As we parted, I knew our paths would never again cross, at least not in any way we could imagine as we searched for our unique paths to enlightenment. I watched him as he walked away from me to enter the temple. I imagined myself in an orange robe, following him, wondering what new insights I might encounter. Yet, I sensed even deeper that the breadth of my life revealed much that he might never experience.

Is that a good thing or not? Enlightenment is in the eye of the beholder, and I prefer my eyes to his, as unwilling to embrace his practice as he is to embrace mine. Even so, we are both on our lifelong paths to our personal nirvana, whatever that may be.

RECOGNITIONS

Quantum Skip

ॐ

I think therefore I am (cogito, ergo sum)
a classic Cartesian dictum in western philosophy
asserts the primacy of consciousness
our mind knowing itself more directly
than it can know the external world

Philosophy cannot rest for long

I am therefore I think (sum, ergo cogito)
a central argument of Sartrean existentialism
asserts existence precedes essence
reality of being is more fundamental
than the emergence of mind

Neither can science rest for long

I feel therefore I am (sentio, ergo sum)
stretches the bounds of rationalism, empiricism
challenges scientific allegiance to Neo-Darwinian materialism
ultimate reality may consist of more peculiarity than imagined
penetrated slowly by our relentless epistemological reach

Stranger than we can imagine

I am therefore I feel and think (cogito ergo sum ergo sentio et)
acknowledges the relativity of phenomenological engagement

with shifting domains of theoretical intelligibility, predictability

revealing ontological features of emergent being

residing even in the quantum skips of consciousness

Schrödinger's cat is purring and not

I am definitely more

than I appear to be

less than I hope to be

Reality no longer

is what it seems

wherever whenever

within and beyond me

This peculiar something

This final mystery

Note 1: The content of this prose is a work in progress and it will arguably never be complete as there is much detail between the lines deserving of further intelligibility in need of a more exhaustive philosophical essay which I invite the reader to write.

Note 2: It is important in the philosophy of science to understand the essential interplay of philosophy and science. In this case, the interplay is between theoretical physics and philosophical metaphysics, even the interplay between knowledge and imagination. There is no clear boundary between the two; rather it is an overlap, a zone filled with tension, well-deserved skepticism, and theoretical failures, affirming the integrity of both science and philosophy. I remain confident that in time our knowledge will grow.

Questions

We need
answers less
questions more
searching ones
prompting us
to think rigorously
reflectively
philosophically

For the incurious mind
questions are unsettling
answers appear superior
presume certainty
For the philosophic mind
answers are unsettling
questions are powerful
presume possibility

One such question
what matters in life
invites abstractions
generates hazy prolixity
framed more meaningfully
how to live a life that matters

invites concrete actions

yielding practical answers

Such a question has

a life of its own

you feel its power

centering our humanity

causing us to wonder

honoring our doubts

resisting easy answers

stretching our imagination

Reflections spawn

penetrating questions

searching further

how to be a better person

how to be authentically human

how to best live and love well

how to enrich our life experiences

how to positively impact the world

Cherish such questions

as close intimate companions

when complications grip us

they become our compass

shred bounds of rationality

enrich our imagination

fortify our resilience

sustain us on our way

Existential questions
take us deeper
into the abyss of consciousness
beyond the edge of the cosmos
why is there something vs. nothing
what is the nature of ultimate reality
what is the nature of being
what is good, just, true, beautiful

Such questions
in our quiet hours
expose ignorance
invite humility
celebrate mystery
revere wonder
intimately nurture
all that is and can be

Even in our best science
most insightful religion
most enduring traditions
unquestioned answers
weigh us down
unanswered questions
propel us forward
into the light of day.

Lightning Rod

ॐ

In my book, *Finding Heart*, I included some philosophical essays focusing primarily on metaphysics and epistemology. They were intentionally parsimonious, leaving much unexplained between the lines. These essays (and some prose) were understandably provocative, and drew immediate commentary, rational and irrational, measured and passionate, from friends and colleagues. As I ponder such, I search for understanding and seek empathy, hoping to learn from others whose views are widely different than my own. To this end, a conceptual typology was invented to differentiate the views of those who are believers versus nonbelievers, and those who are moderately accommodating of my views versus those who are antithetically opposed to them.

First, the religious believers, who are antithetically opposed to my views, argue that my skepticism runs too deep, invites nihilism, and prevents open-mindedness to religious sentience, if not religious authority and tradition. They cite my prose focusing mostly on dark existential matters, especially suffering and death. They strongly resist my atheistic sojourns. To test my open-mindedness, I invite them to share personal religious experiences or reasons for religious belief. I hear fewer stories than expected of mystical or miraculous experiences, but when I do, mostly inexplicably incredible encounters are reported. It is in these encounters with emotive significance beneath the invention of cognitive explanation that a person appears moved to embrace a life of faith. For me, this is what *finding heart* is all about. Of course, there are those who examine my book briefly and decline to read it, perhaps wanting to add it to the book burning pile. I hear words such as infidel, heretic, antichrist, and blasphemer—labels which are dismissive and void of understanding. Such believers tend to draw their circle to shut me out, whereas I draw my circle to take them in.

Second, across the philosophical courtyard are the defiant nonbelievers, generally atheists. In contrast to believers, they argue that my hopefulness is too generous and is ultimately delusional. They encourage me to honor my skepticism first and foremost; I agree with them. They point to an otherwise unfriendly universe, to the pervasive suffering and injustice absorbed by humanity, to the "absence of evidence" revealing an "evidence of absence" (of God) in our lives. They view religion as mostly wishful placation and frequently toxic to rationality. I invite them to entertain the possibility that we might be locked inside a dispositional box which precludes us from being sensitive to the wonder and mystery of existence, that the unknown may hold a few surprises for us, that some aspects of religious experience may reveal such to us. Again, that is what *finding heart* is all about. Of course, there are those in this camp who briefly examine my book and dismiss it as gentle "softheaded" agnosticism.

Third, there are believers who are moderately tolerant of my views. Some view my deep skepticism as an unfortunate original philosophical bias, whereas others view my hopefulness as a precursor to a more compelling faith. They draw their philosophical circle widely to include me, and I truly enjoy inclusion. They prefer to be in a space of loving kindness, accepting me for who I am, in spite of my questioning attitude, and focus on the virtues of our relationship. Any serious conversation, however, often leads to consideration of a willing suspension of doubts. I suggest that a stronger faith may evolve from confronting dissonance and deception underlying religious convictions. Not a comfortable prospect for most. However, *finding heart* appears to emerge more often here. Most in this camp read my book, and empathize with my reflections and stories.

Fourth, there are non-believers who are moderately accommodating of my view as a hopeful skeptic, generally agnostics. Without compromising their philosophical posture, they hover on the edge of theoretical physics and flirt with metaphysics. They are willing to acknowledge the possibility of unknown aspects of reality beyond our current comprehension, but not likely God in any form close to what is traditionally posed by religion. While they respect my hopefulness, they cannot embrace it fully, as there is insufficient evidence to warrant possibility. In fact, they assert that I am really an agnostic with a mystic's mantle, and that my definition of agnosticism is too tight, i.e., believing that you cannot know, only that you do not know about the veracity of metaphysical propositions. I suspect that *finding heart* is present, too. Some in this camp read my book, and hold their philosophical reservations in abeyance, unshared.

I wish I could say that it is enjoyable to bring such spirited people together for a discussion. Being a moderator is one thing, but too often

I am a referee. Inevitably, they are compelled to argue their points of view, and stop listening to each other after a brief period of tolerance, unwilling to allow facts to interfere with the truth. Only with the passage of time, do they become more willing to listen, occasionally experiencing an awakening of being the cause of their own eclipse.

It gets really interesting when I assert that being a *hopeful skeptic* is not about balancing opposing views and finding middle ground. On the contrary, it is a moral imperative to completely and authentically honor intellectual integrity and expunge nonsense, and continue to sharpen critical thinking, while seeking to broaden and deepen the range of *possibility*. A humble recognition of ignorance is healthy, given the deep mystery of existence, the limits of our scientific paradigms and epistemological reach, the relative insignificance of our place in the cosmos, and the overriding value of life itself. Life is more meaningful when I inhale *possibility* with my first breath each day, and ultimately and intimately seek to *find heart* with my last breath.

As you read this account, you may find yourself mostly identifying with one of the four types of *crossfire*. Reading descriptors may speak to you deeply, recognizing your own philosophical sojourns and biases. I invite you in the midst of this crossfire, to empathize with more than one of the others. If you do, I promise you that there may be more than a few insightful surprises awaiting you in the midst of philosophical crossfire.

Becoming a Hopeful Skeptic

ॐ

De omnibus disputandum. (Rene Descartes)

Skeptics are at home in philosophical and scientific circles but are often marginalized in society, especially in religious communities. Among them are defiant atheists and inpatient agnostics who broadly embrace skepticism, reflecting a general hostility toward metaphysics and religion. However, skepticism is more philosophically robust, reflecting surprising sensitivity to meaning arising out of the human condition. While its moral imperative demands rigorous, searching analysis, it ultimately entails a simple search for truth. In sum, skeptics are *nonbelievers* until otherwise convinced.

How do we know what is so?

The arguments of nonbelievers (skeptics) and believers (religionists) collide in a heated debate over the nature of knowledge, belief and opinion, questions which reside in the philosophical domain of epistemology. Skeptics affirm knowledge only after rigorous rational research and analysis produces credible evidence, rooted in logical empiricism. Their epistemological capacity and reach are well defined, albeit mostly by science. When they are presented with an idea or argument, their initial response is: *Show me the evidence!* In the absence of evidence, *good faith doubt* becomes the skeptic's firewall against nonsense in all forms, not just religious. Skeptics reject alternative theories (sources) of knowledge such as sentient experiences because of marginal objectivity and credibility.

Believers, conversely, affirm mystical and miraculous experiences as generating religious knowledge beyond the reach of science. They view the scientific paradigm as narrow in scope and lose confidence and patience with its limited and incomplete view of reality. They opt for existential clarity and certainty, albeit faith-based. They are quick to move from speculation to formal belief to absolute truth. Religion may become an ersatz for science. Some believers acknowledge this tendency and confess their reservations, yet argue there is sufficient reason (if not evidence) to believe and make a leap of faith.

Both skeptics and believers ponder the nature of reality and ask: *Why is there something rather than nothing?* Exploring this fundamental question can be confounding to both. Just maybe both our science and religion are primitive in scope, each inching toward a better understanding of reality.

What do we actually know for sure?

The widening gap between skeptics and believers unfortunately polarizes and often radicalizes the human mind. Both assert *truth claims* and accuse each other of being the cause of their own eclipse (ignorance or falsehood). Evidentiary criteria appear stronger for the skeptic who relies upon empirical verification and consensual validation, whereas believers rely upon subjective experiences, asserted as authentic, but raising issues of reliability and credibility. Undaunted, believers invoke *faith* as a defense. And skeptics champion *doubt* as an offense. And the missiles fly, wounding both parties!

Most skeptics are circumspect of their bounded rationality and judgment biases. They remain skeptical in the face of insufficient credible evidence for metaphysical assertions, not just those from religion. However, they apply the same evidentiary standard to their own views, acknowledging a sweeping negation (e.g., no God in any form) is untenable. Atheists disagree, arguing that *the absence of evidence is evidence of absence*. Skeptics embrace the view of an unfriendly, indeterminate universe and a marginal human condition, in which there is little evidence of *supernatural* phenomenon or little need to invent such ideas for explanatory purposes. In the face of competing explanations, the simplest complete theory is most likely the best one. However, skeptics can be inconsistent, e.g. recognize the mystery of quantum gravity or covariant quantum fields in theoretical physics, but trivialize the mystery of consciousness (and qualia) and summarily dismiss alternative metaphysical sojourns beyond the edge of science. Skeptics need to be circumspect of their own leaps of faith, and to resist knowing for sure, in the face of equivocality; there is a huge difference between an untested theory and one with a history of overwhelming research and evidence.

Most believers want to know for sure. Their deepest impulse informs them of God providing such knowledge by sentient experiences, sacred script, ancient traditions, and most importantly, life experience, e.g. evidence of design thus a designer (teleological argument). Some openly admit that their religious knowledge is subjective and even equivocal, but that in and of itself, does not invalidate its truthfulness nor should it be marginalized because of uncertainty. Making a leap of faith entails suspending such reservations in favor of a religious life. Believers tend to assert: *I don't need to see the evidence until it presents itself; in its absence, I am willing to make a choice to believe.*

What is wrong with saying: I don't know?

Navigating this philosophical landscape is tricky and filled with ethical and epistemological quagmires. While skeptics vehemently challenge the metaphysical assertions of believers, they openly confess to their own ignorance of the unknown, albeit growing in scope, and a constant need to revise theories in the face of advancing scientific research and evidence. The nature of science is slowly progressive and painstakingly prudent. Skeptics smile when confessing: *We simply don't know.* They frown when acknowledging that they also don't know whether salient experiences can be authentic and a source of knowledge, beyond the reach of science. For the believer, however, their philosophical space is more unstable, as they seldom confess of being wrong or in doubt. To do so may be an act of heresy.

I personally reject the assumptions and dogma of both camps, embracing *good faith doubt* to move into more reasonable philosophical space. My skepticism runs very deep, also being my intellectual default option. In my view, it serves the interests of both believer and nonbeliever. Arguments asserting the truth value of metaphysical and ethical propositions must be subjected to rigorous, critical philosophical analysis. It is a simple moral imperative. Reality can be confounding, straining the capacity of our best search for knowledge. In the end, *if we don't know something, we admit it; if we claim to know something, we demonstrate it. If we cannot, but contingently elect to believe it, we are honest about such faith.* We resist speculatively filling in the blanks in our metaphysical puzzle. Again, the wisdom of Carl Sagan echoes, "extraordinary claims require extraordinary evidence." Otherwise, our assertions are mere wishful conjectures or elaborate metaphysical systems or well-developed scientific theories, awaiting confirmation or disconfirmation. Such skepticism fortifies intellectual and moral integrity. It should be respected as reasonable and not breached by even our best intentions.

What is right about saying: I hope so?

Preserving open-mindedness and intellectual integrity becomes salient in the face of torturous skepticism and dogmatic religion. An inquisitive mind is valued, full of curiosity, and open to surprise. Given this learning perspective, it is unreasonable to summarily reject the *possibility of more going on (or not) in both the human condition and the universe*, while affirming, not denying reservations about it. In other words, be skeptical first and foremost by honoring *good faith doubt*, yet embrace possible grounds for *hope*. Revere the unknown, the deep mystery around us, as a source of existential wonder and surprise, acknowledging that our best science and religion does not completely understand it. Take a breath! Remain prudently sensitive to the faithful impulses of believers and to the doubtful impulses of skeptics.

Becoming *a hopeful skeptic* resists intellectual foreclosure regarding the *possibility* of a friendly universe. Prevailing scientific perspectives can be held in abeyance, allowing a leap of curiosity and faith that just maybe ultimate reality is more complex and peculiar, beyond our current capability of detecting or even imagining it. The skeptic smiles at this slim chance but is humbly reminded of being ignorantly wrong. In the end, being a seeker of truth with an open mind is a good thing, maybe the best of things!

As a hard-core skeptic with a modest dose of hopefulness, it is good to be more respectful of the metaphysical and spiritual sojourns of believers, and suggest that reflective thinking could nurture a stronger faith among us. In sum, believers could consider *good doubt faith* as contrasted with *good faith doubt,* entertaining doubts about religious metaphysics as reasonable and not diminishing faith. Imagine hopeful skeptics and doubtful believers actually talking to each other, reconsidering their respective arguments, suspending their hostilities, and even engaging in common humanitarian efforts together. We may spare each other the rancorous rhetoric of radicalized views on both ends of this debate, and all of the hate, mean-spiritedness, and anger that typically ensues. Shame on us if we persist! We might even become less concerned about metaphysics, and more focused on ethics and the pursuit of a virtuous life. Imagine that! We may *seek and find heart!* We may even come to like each other.

Being a skeptic who has had inexplicable mystical experiences, I have good reason to pause and ponder my paradigmatic bounds and most cherished assumptions, even if I have no idea as to what is being revealed to me or if it is existentially authentic. Admittedly, such salient experiences may be attributable to plausible naturalistic explanations. Even so, my consciousness is deepened by such experiences, inviting possible insight or delusion or both. Atheists are quick to point this out. When such experiences lead to diverse competing religious' truth claims across various cultures around the world (4,200 religions), issues of credibility understandably arise, generating enormous dissonance. In this maze, both hope and doubt are good things for believer and skeptic alike.

I suspect there is a *philosopher* deep within you somewhere, napping perhaps, or preoccupied with irrelevant nonsense, or writing a comic strip, or watching an incredible sunset, inviting you to join in this philosophical dance, to reflect critically on your beliefs and non-beliefs, whether believer or skeptic or undecided, to honor both hope and doubt, and most importantly, *to seek and find heart* in this incredible life journey.

Note: Final Truth, In Praise of Doubt, and In Praise of Hope are related reflections in my first book, *Finding Heart* (2012).

It Is What It Is

ॐ

Life happens. We may be prepared for what happens. We may not be. No worries. We may learn more when unprepared. It may be painful and unfair.

Change is the only constant. It is inevitable. We may initiate it or be surprised by it. Unpredictability and impermanence rule. You may like it or not.

It is what it is.

We want life to be different. It ought to be better. It should be, could be, can be. Things happen for a reason, or things happen for no reason at all.

We want to be different. We may like ourselves or not. We struggle to be better. We may be able to influence personal change. We may not.

It is what it is.

Time moves on. A steady, relentless pace. Our human journey moves with it. We cannot slow it down. Yesterday is gone. A part of our lives is gone forever.

The unknown is far greater than the known. Our ignorance is far greater than our knowledge. We are alive and here. That we know. This is what matters.

It is what it is.

A new day starts. The sun shines or the rain falls. Bad things happen to good people. Good things happen to bad people. The universe is unfair.

We grow old. We grow weak. Our health fails. We die. We wonder if this is the end. We don't know. We may hope for the best, and fear the worst.

It is what it is.

We watch children grow and stumble. We wish to prevent their heartaches. We cannot love without such pain. Such pain may be the reason we love.

We lose some of them. We cannot prevent it. It is not our fault. We search for the courage to move on. We may not find it. The wind is cold.

It is what it is.

Religion as Art

Considering religion as *art* is an intriguing idea. And a promising one, too. Religious practitioners have much in common with artists, expressing what they feel deeply, in various forms, and endeavoring to enrich the world through their practice. Religion would arguably be refocused by such a paradigm shift. To explore this idea further, one option is to consider its similarities within the conceptual framework of faith, imagination, conscience, and community.

Art first and foremost requires *faith,* as does religion. An artist has aesthetic experiences which are emotional, spiritual, inspirational, and mystical in nature, revealing a sense of purpose and promise, revealing insights beyond our senses. Religious experience is also essentially aesthetic. It is highly subjective and private, often inexplicable yet indelible, allowing expression only through artistry (worship or practice). Given the diverse expressions of artistry *and* the diverse emergence of over 4,200 religions in the world, one could arguably consider religion as an art form.

Faith, however, has a dark side. It is imperative for people of faith to be circumspect of its adverse effects. It can promote ignorance, where the turtle withdraws into its shell. Science and education may be devalued in a worldview constructed only by faith alone, in which only scriptures and rites are emphasized as a source of knowledge. Radicalized cults especially reflect this tendency.

Art requires *imagination*. Artists are compelled to express their faith in what they imagine. A visual artist clearly has a vision which is conveyed to the canvass and invites the viewer to "experience" its unique expression and impact. We may view it as appealing or unappealing to our aesthetic sense. A musical composer may similarly use innovative forms and styles which are appealing or unappealing. Poetry may speak to us deeply or merely place us in intellectual slumber. Dance may release us into a mystical space of profound vibrancy and spontaneity, or it may merely encumber our senses. I imagine a beautiful ballet with a scenic backdrop with music by Mozart; to me, a truly religious experience. People of faith share much in common with artists who embrace aesthetic imagination in artwork, literature, poetry, music, theater, and dance. In religion, imagination is most typically expressed metaphysically in the form of speculation about God, creation, afterlife, the universe, and the nature of ultimate reality. In a very real sense, these speculations are artistic expressions, whose meaning resides in the artist.

Imagination also has a dark side. Religion can speculate about what is ultimately real, and elevate it to the status of absolute truth and dogma. Attempting to explain religious experience is to be expected by a person of faith; however, such explanations tend to be speculative. Worse yet, religious believers may be criticized as having insufficient faith when they fail to ascribe truth status to speculations. Skeptics raise their defiant voices whenever religion becomes an ersatz for science and philosophy. Rather than compete with science, religion and science could complement each other. Viewing religion as an *art* would enhance this possibility. Moreover, we can focus on the experience of being religious and of sensing the sacred in nature and humanity. Theists who make factual claims about the nature of reality are at risk of lacking credibility and empirical verifiability, fueling an on-going debate about faith and reason, leading to an unfortunate polarization between believers and nonbelievers. While it is healthy for religious believers to imagine how the universe works, and to embrace it in nurturing faith, it is risky to view such speculations as absolute truth.

To shift religion to an aesthetic paradigm does not require an absence of metaphysical propositions. Religious imagination is clearly expressive of deeply emotional yearnings in which our being reaches into the mystery of existence and senses what may or may not be real. Believers are *religious artists*, expressing in more tangible forms what their underlying spiritual experiences reveal to them. Within this paradigm, religion is not immune to criticism, any more than art is immune to literary or artistic criticism, but standards are much different than the rigorous ones required of science.

Art requires *conscience.* An artist searches for purpose underlying expression, often invoking modest moral preferences. The rest of us have the opportunity to experience their artistry. As we do, we are emotionally affected from inspirational awe to existential angst. Religion becomes art when we imagine the good that we can create in the world, even our private world. We develop the will to act in the service of others. It is pure reflection and persistent action in virtuous living. It not only follows light, it generates light, holding our torch high, shining through the darkness around us. Art is not rational nor need it be. When we hear a beautiful symphony or view a beautiful work of art, we never think of it in rational terms, only aesthetically. Religion recognizes that the natural world and humanity can reveal such beauty and goodness to us. Religion helps us to see it, experience it fully, and contribute to the conditions that create and sustain it.

Conscience, too, has a dark side. It can foster self-righteousness, moral superiority, and ugly contempt. You may think your farts smell better than others. They don't! Moral absolutes are not absolute! Conversely, moral relativism is overly ambiguous and confounding. Seeking moral high ground is a good idea, but cannot ignore the low ground of competing moral interests and preferences. Most art tends to honor moral diversity across cultures. In my view, it is morally irresponsible to impose moral standards on people, on the grounds that theirs are inferior. Living in a democratic society with constitutional rights to life, liberty, and the pursuit of happiness, I intend to resist the moral tyranny and narcissism of others imposing their moral will upon me. I can make my moral choices, and others can make theirs, and we can live in peace without righteous violence toward each other.

Conscience has an even deeper dark side. In religion, it may move to sermons filled with radicalized politics, promoting hatred and violence. It tears us down rather than lifting us up! In art, we sense what is and is not aesthetically appealing. We know good art when we see it, and move past other art, recognizing that beauty is in the eye of the beholder. You are a jury of one and only one, no more. Progressive democratic societies promote the arts and protect their religions.

Art requires *community*. Art requires faith, discipline, and practice. It also requires an audience just as a minister requires a congregation. Art requires a concert hall or theater or art gallery or street corner. Religion as art deserves both private and public expression. For the religious believer, it is not enough to simply believe, for their faith compels them to act in creating goodness and compassion toward others. It is primarily at the level of religious community that efforts are initiated to *seek and find heart*.

Community has a dark side. It can be exclusive and become isolated. It can construct a dark sense of social reality unique to a particular art or religious community in which only the needs of members are served. In such cases, we may be stripped of humanitarian concerns and actions. Visual artists may ignore the work of performing or literary artists, just as liberally minded congregations and radicalized conservative religious communities may avoid outreach to each other. Religion may suffer from the narcissism of minor differences in doctrine or practice.

I tend to resist religion in its most traditional and contemporary forms. However, I find ample room in my weary old skeptic mind for religion as art, as a sincere effort to create good in the world and to pay homage to the sacred when it appears. So, on this dark, rainy day, as I walk with a homeless person to buy him a cup of coffee, as he shares his appreciation and I share mine (think about it), I am being religious in bringing goodness into his life and mine. As I contribute resources to a humanitarian foundation, but also volunteer to contribute my time and energy in working on projects, I am being religious. While I prefer the term "philosophical" to religious, I want to draw my circle sufficiently wide to include my religiously faithful friends. Why bicker over minor differences when pursuing a good life?

Some say that religious faith is a willing suspension of disbelief. I disagree. Religion as *art* honors doubt. It entails suspension of speculation about reality, inviting a leap in the direction of creating goodness in the world. No need to sit in church for any purpose other than inspiration to do good, and then get up, get out, and get on with it in a respectful and sensible manner. One is less likely to *find heart,* sitting in a church.

This short essay is merely intended to invite a conversation about "religion as art." It falls short of discussing a full range of issues involved in this discussion. Before we explore those further, however, just faithfully imagine that you are an *artist* who is creating an *artwork* by your religious faith and life.

On Religious Epistemology

☙

The following short essay is framed as a *"fable"* to illustrate the issues surrounding the search for and construction of religious knowledge.

Imagine an isolated island, distant from other land. Imagine its inhabitants believe in the existence of a white sparrow with miraculous power, somewhere on the island. Many revere and worship it, believing it is sacred. You are open to belief, but decide to search for the sparrow first, seeking experience of whether the sparrow exists.

You begin your search. You are excited with anticipation. You walk around the island. You remain still, looking and listening for the white sparrow. Distractions are avoided. Silence prevails, except for gusts of wind and rushes of incoming surf. You look for movement among the trees, bushes, grass, and clouds. No sightings occur. You listen. You hear nothing, though you may not recognize its sound. Others have similar experiences. The sparrow appears to be absent. This absence in and of itself is not confirmation that the sparrow is not on the island; only that it is not near you. Lack of movement and sound are only evidence of non-discovery, for the sparrow may prefer to be out of range, and even if present, may avoid detection. For one to assert that the white sparrow does not exist, the entire island would have to be systematically searched with sufficient controls to ensure that it is not moving around or hiding. A sweeping negation of its existence is indeed problematic, whereas its affirmation arguably requires only specific empirical evidence.

You have an extraordinary experience; the sparrow appears to be in your large coat pocket. You reach into your pocket and can "feel" its softness and warmth. You may even feel its heart beating. You alone may hear it. However, you cannot pull it out of your pocket for others to see because it is likely to escape and fly away. You can only tell others that you "feel" the presence of the sparrow and believe it is in your pocket, that you now "know" the sparrow exists. You describe how it feels: soft, warm, alive, peaceful, and "like" a sparrow. Others report similar experiences. Without question, you are convinced. To support your conviction, you begin experiencing sightings or sounds, but not with concurrent validation and consensus of others in the same exact circumstances.

Time passes on the island. Some people report "feeling" the sparrow and "witnessing" such, whereas others believe such reports, albeit with no direct sentient experience. Faith arises. Doubt arises, too. Perhaps, what one experienced was not the white sparrow after all. The extraordinary experience may have a more plausible explanation. Perhaps, one was so convinced that a white sparrow existed, that their mind played an unfortunate trick on them. Doubts may interfere with faith. To initially form faith, one needs only to believe based on the *witness* of others until confirmatory experience arises, if and when it does. Faith may set doubts aside.

Despite naysayers, others remain convinced that there is a white sparrow. They engage in practices of search (and worship), reporting even the slightest movements or sounds or internal impulses. They begin to elaborate on its nature: very quick, mysterious, perhaps invisible, even supernatural. There is only one white sparrow according to most believers. The sparrow seems to defy detection. It may even defy description. Over time, rich traditions, historic scripts, and folklore emerge to assert the existence of the white sparrow. People believe it has the power to help them to do good and resist evil. People come to revere the sparrow, even though they may not have directly witnessed it. They may choose to simply believe. They make a leap of faith.

It seems the nature of the sparrow may surpass our comprehension. Others wonder how such an amazing entity with such an incredible power and impact on our lives, can remain so undetected. Maybe it lives outside the island. Believers counter that the effect of the sparrow is sufficient evidence of its existence. But, the effects appear to be mostly random, inconsistent and equivocal. In the end, we cannot even *know* that the sparrow is white, has wings, or can fly. We may come to realize that a leap of humble doubt may be our most genuine act of religious faith. Or not.

Faith in the sparrow only requires a willing suspension of disbelief and a robust imagination. In sum, start *sensing* its presence. Such sentience is ultimately subjective, and subjectivity is problematic, for the sensation may not be genuine or accurate. Of course, it may be.

Integrity requires a willing suspension of such speculation and respect for reasonable doubt and prudence. It does not, however, preclude faith.

Imagine there is no white sparrow. What then? A question that many may wish to simply avoid. Maybe in the absence of knowledge and in the presence of ignorance, we remain humble, open-minded seekers, using faith to sustain us. Maybe we acknowledge that there is much about the island we don't know and may never know, and entertain the possibility that there is more going on than we imagine or ever can imagine. Maybe we resist converting speculations about what we really don't know into what we wish we could know. Maybe we focus on the ethical and cultural grounding of virtuous living, pursuing what matters most in life and endeavoring to achieve the greatest good for humanity in our tiny corner of the universe.

Or maybe we don't, and we continue to wander and wonder.

Crossfire on Campus

ೞ

Walking to my university office today, the campus was alive with political protests and demonstrations along with an array of community and student interest booths. One booth that I had not previously noticed, was called "Students with Non-Religious Views." Two large signs were prominently displayed: "Don't Believe in God? You Are Not Alone!" and "We Don't Attack Religion. We Provide an Alternative!" Words like atheist and agnostic were conspicuously absent. Some students were drawn to the booth, whereas others avoided it completely. The student traffic pattern seemed to reflect the popularized views on religion in our society. I stopped to talk to the students, praising them for providing alternative views, and for openly bringing like-minded students together. As I did, I heard someone shout "antichrist!" An older adult with a bible in hand shouted "Burn in Hell!" No worry, they resisted a response and continued our polite conversation.

In moments such as this one, I confess to philosophically admiring our First Amendment. Free speech is essential in a healthy political democracy, as is a free press and the right of assembly and movement. I am unabashed about my advocacy of these rights, especially when others express opinions different than my own, or when well-meaning moralists attempt to censor expression. The redeeming value in such freedom is that we may learn from each other in ways that surprise and inform us, leading to new insights. The university campus thrives on academic freedom and a robust intellectual exchange.

As I sit on a bench to enjoy a quick lunch, several professors and students get into a debate about religion. No surprise as such engagement is what defines a university. I eventually join in, suggesting middle ground between the popularized views. My comments are ignored, as most seem interested in only advocating their respective views. Rising passions ignite a crossfire of opinions and emotions.

Student A: I am an atheist, and I am glad that an alternative exists on campus, though I don't have time to get involved in it. Frankly, we need a place for non-religious students to enjoy each other. Given the various religious groups on campus, it is time for atheists to come out of the closet and be acknowledged.

Student B: Wouldn't it be like forming your own secular church? Instead of the Bible, you would read Dawkins and Harris, and bash those of us who believe in God. In fact, your god is an intellectual black hole.

Professor A: I don't think critical thinking entails "bashing." Rather, it is a commitment to intelligibility and common sense. I would invite both theists and atheists to express their views in a civil manner, and maybe we can grow to understand each other better.

Student C: What is there to understand about atheists, other than they think that Christians like me, are delusional and disingenuous. Religious faith doesn't have to be subjected to academic scrutiny. My belief in

God is unwavering, and I resent people challenging my faith and portraying me as intellectually compromised.

Student A: You have described yourself fairly well! Add self-deception and self-righteousness to your list.

Student B: Go to hell!

Student D: You guys are ready to fight before we have begun to talk sensibly. I'm sure that not even God is happy with such a response.

I find myself acting mostly as a facilitator, intervening to limit interruptions and personal attacks. Given the fierce polemics, a better descriptor of my role is "referee," and I struggle in maintaining the focus on attacking ideas, not people.

Professor B: Ok, the real issue here is how we form our beliefs about anything. If we rely on empirical evidence, then our beliefs tend to be credible. But, if we rely on alternative forms of evidence such as religious script or authority, then we end up with conflicting beliefs. The world is filled with different religions, each of whom believes they have an exclusive corner on truth value.

Student C: Look, I don't need to critically examine my belief in God. It is what it is. I simply choose to believe, and I don't rely on empirical evidence beyond what I sense within myself. God is revealed within us, not out there, and certainly not through science. Atheists are blind to this type of religious experience.

Student D: I'm an agnostic and proud of it! I went to church as a kid, but I just couldn't bring myself to believe what my parents believed. Because of that, my parents have cut me off completely. Is that an act of Christian charity?

Student A: What annoys me about the two of you (B & C) is that you probably ignore important political issues, such as environmental quality and community health. It seems that your time would be better spent involved in addressing these issues, rather than sitting in church or reading the bible.

Professor A: That may be a bias! I attend church occasionally, and the minister appears to be very concerned about environmental quality, encouraging the congregation to not pollute air and water and to conserve energy.

Student D: Those sermons are meaningless if not accompanied by action. Does your minister encourage members to join environmental protection groups? I suspect not.

Student C: Let God worry about environmental quality. There are more pressing moral issues such as protecting human life at conception and protecting the sanctity of marriage. We need to address these fundamental ethical issues.

Student A: Moral issues are such a big deal to religious zealots. Abortion and gay marriage should be non-issues, especially when compared to environmental quality, public health, gun control, immigration, and human rights—to name just a few.

Professor B: Maybe we can explore middle ground to find a way to resolve even the moral issues?

Professor A: Like burn down abortion clinics? (little laughter)

Professor B: What if we could agree to abortions in limited cases such as rape or life-threatening cases, and ban abortions resulting from consensual sex?

Most Students: We cannot agree to that. (Students B & C: murder is murder!) (Students A & D: A woman should have the right to decide!)

Student A: The entire idea of a democracy is that we have the freedom to form our own moral values as long as they don't harm others, and not be constricted to a single narrow moral or religious perspective. What if I took the position that our society needs to limit population growth, thus no couple can have more than two children. If a woman with two children becomes pregnant, then she is required to have an abortion. That moral posture is not much different than the one adopted by right to life advocates.

Professor B: Ok, let's agree to disagree on that issue. One of you commented that we should let God worry about the environment. What did you mean by that?

Student C: I believe that we are in the last days of this planet. The time is at hand for the second coming of Christ, and before that can happen, we will be in a state of worldwide chaos and destruction.

Student A: That is so much religious BS! And even if it were remotely true, wouldn't God want us to protect the environment?

Student C: Not really. He would want us to do everything we could to hasten the decline of the environment.

Professor A: Are you serious? Are you saying that the sooner we destroy our environment, the sooner the second coming of Christ will happen?

Student C: That's how I see it.

Student B: I totally disagree. I am a religious believer. I believe that God expects us to protect the earth, and any actions that diminish that are basically evil.

Student D: I love it when true believers cannot agree on such a fundamental moral issue. It is obvious that your ethical perspective is screwed up by religion.

Student E: Religion poisons everything—politics, families, emotional well-being, etc. My god is the university! Education trumps ignorance! Why do we continue to embrace the beliefs of a tribe of nomads wandering in the desert during the Stone Age?

Students B & C: (in unison) You are your own problem; if you don't get religion, it's because you are not strong enough to get it, not willing to take a leap of faith.

Professor A: My concern is radicalization! It seems that more polarization leads to increased radicalization and the emergence of extreme views. At that point, we stop listening and start fighting.

An hour has passed, and students begin to leave for classes. A small group of professors remain. We have an enduring hope that this "crossfire" was a positive experience, that learning actually occurred. Even so, we wonder if we could find a way to promote respect for each other's points of view, without succumbing to stereotypes and prejudice. That task will have to wait for another day, as we shake hands and go our separate ways.

Returning to my office, a student knocks on my door to invite me to speak to the "Students with Non-Religious Views" group. I agree to do so with the understanding that I am free to select my topic and format.

Vital Narcissistic Lies

C&

I know everything

I need to know,

believe me, I do.

Just ask me,

I will tell you

all you need to know,

trust me, I will.

I truly enjoy

our similar views.

You seem to know

what I know. We are

better together,

learn so much

from each other.

Others know less,

get it very wrong

with fictions, not facts.

We can only smile

at their stupidity,

at our brilliance,

knowing truth alone.

On Courage

ॐ

(notes for my grandchildren)

Rafting and kayaking rivers in my life were incredible adventures, evoking vivid memories of beautiful landscapes and challenging whitewater rapids. Such feats took skill, endurance, and a modest dose of *courage* coping with the fear of *heading down into it*. Most serious rapids were well scouted and carefully navigated, but unpredictable unknowns and serious risks were always inescapable; indeed, the "spice" in my adventures.

"Running Rivers" evoke a metaphor of navigating our moral landscape in life, addressing challenging moral choices and conflicts, complicated by unpredictable circumstances, requiring our best judgment, and in the end, requiring *courage*. Confronting a moral dilemma is much like standing at the top of a Class V rapid, scouting it out, identifying its various hazards, and planning a course to navigate it successfully. Otherwise, we are at serious risk of life-threatening mishaps. *It takes courage to protect and fortify our moral integrity, and be clear-headed about our underlying ethical philosophy.* Courage to not only enter the flow of moral choices and head *into it*, but courage to recognize that the river is much more powerful than we, and must be respected. Philosophers devote much thought (ethics) to critically examining competing moral interests and to resolving ethical conflicts and ambiguities. If self-interests alone dominate, we may "jump in the river and head into it" without much ethical forethought about the interests of others in the raft and possible adverse impacts upon the natural environment. In life, we need to develop moral clarity and resolve, related decisional skills, and have resources to fortify us.

Mountain climbing, incredible adventures in my lifetime, evoke lasting memories of grandeur and serenity. Risks were always present: sheer vertical exposure, blue ice, loose rock, high winds, extreme weather, crevasses, and avalanches. The taunting philosophic question persisted: Why climb it? Unlike rivers, mountaineering took tremendous conditioning, skill, endurance, and time. It was not for the fainthearted who didn't like sweat and exhaustion.

"Climbing Mountains" provides a helpful metaphor, though different from rivers: *Rather than heading down into it, I am heading up out of it, often to a summit.* To me, the *courage* required is similar to what is needed to strengthen our *intellectual integrity.* We decide not only the types of knowledge to place in our brains, but also hopefully recognize that supposed knowledge may not be what it seems: certain and unequivocal. To test the quality of knowledge demands allegiance to philosophical analysis: critical thinking, sound argumentation, and good judgment. Our culture surrounds us with much disinformation, nonsense, and confusion. It takes a keen intellect to recognize such, and muster the *courage to confront it directly,* to be a relentless fact finder and checker, and to expose self-deception and delusion. Just as climbing a mountain requires impeccable research and resolve to successfully attempt the ascent, intellectual integrity is not much different. It requires vigilance and courage in resisting what threatens it.

Day-to-day "horizontal" adventures are also fulfilling. Rather than evoking inspirational metaphors, their relevance rests in the stories they inspire. For most of my adult life, I enjoyed distance running, participating in road runs, including marathons. However, distance running took much more than merely showing up to run a race: a rigorous running schedule, strength training, diet, stretching, and adequate rest. Beyond all else, it took *courage* to remain disciplined in spite of competing interests and demands.

My stories of distance running are not nearly as exciting as river running and mountain climbing but are salient to *political integrity*. The *courage* required for political advocacy and activism is much different: resilience, endurance, strength, patience, persistence, and civil disobedience. A truly democratic society attempts to preserve human liberty and promote legal, economic, and social justice. It only works if you work to sustain it! It requires political debate, action, protest, and elections. It also requires resistance to tyranny, radicalization, anarchy, and civil violence. You may become weary of such activism, giving in to apathy and cynicism, believing that an individual cannot make a difference. You are wrong; you can. More importantly, you must! It takes *courage* first and foremost to hold the torch high and remain active in important political causes.

The same *courage* is essential for *well-being integrity*, emotionally and physically. When persons or circumstances place us at serious risk or harm. it takes courage to resist such. To fortify such courage, it is essential to strengthen emotional and social intelligence (EQ). Recognize when you are stuck in a static, low progress mode of allowing a single form of work or entertainment or inactivity to dominate your life (e.g., gaming, sports, TV or movies, artistic endeavors). Life balance is essential in promoting your well-being.

You will never do anything in this world without courage. (Aristotle)

No philosopher or poet has ever claimed that *courage* is an easily developed or sustainable virtue. It may be one of the most challenging and difficult, requiring the confidence and resilience to fight for what really matters in life, especially our *moral, intellectual, political and well-being integrity*. It requires good judgment, to pick and fight our battles well, sometimes in the face of overwhelming odds. We cannot wait to first develop confidence to assert courage; rather assert courage first, and confidence will grow. Live *a courageous life*, even when heartaches and failures haunt you. If you do, you will enjoy self-respect, a warm realization in the quiet hours of your life.

Alone

ॐ

Alone, I am at risk of being lonely. In my early life, I avoided being alone to avoid such risk. No one likes being lonely. A complete waste. Dead spacetime. Nonbeing. Existential black hole. Nearly extinction. The absolute worst of what life offers. *Stop!* Time to get a grip. Time to wake up and take a breath. I pause and listen to my self-talk: mostly positive or negative? Am I my own best friend or own worst enemy?

Over the course of my life, I increasingly sought time to be alone, even welcoming loneliness. I suspect you may have done likewise. Of course, there were times when it would sneak up on me. Even so, the "best friend" in me would embrace social isolation as an opportunity for emotional nutrition, a gift to enhance my well-being. I gave myself the space to meditate on so much: *memories, accomplishments, adventures, dreams, and especially, reflective philosophical thoughts.* As I did, I discovered my life is a rich colorful tapestry of existential encounters, generating meaning, purpose, and promise. My meditations led to newly discovered insights, to reliving experiences and noticing detail previously unnoticed, and to initiate a quiet, private celebration of what matters most in my life. My aloneness became a mystic portal to *finding heart.*

One interesting insight in my "alone times" is that it was one thing to celebrate my most cherished relationships with people, but quite another to overanalyze them. If issues existed, it was much more preferable to engage a person directly about such, rather than vault such thoughts away for another day. I would simply flag them and move on in my meditative deliberations. I would not allow myself to get stuck in the negative energy of dysfunctional relationships because they mostly required fresh air together.

Another option alone was to lift myself up out of meditation and think deeply about key topics of philosophical interest, not personal issues. I invited *old friends* (authors of favorite books) into my inner conversation, imagining them talking to me, sharing their wisdom. I would take reflective walks or hikes into serene places, in beautiful city parks or along rivers, allowing my mind to reflect without distraction. My cellphone was shut off! Such sojourns did not need a particular destination or itinerary, nor did my journey require a predetermined direction. No rush, no worries.

Often, it was even better to not fill my mind with thoughts, recognizing that it was more therapeutic to simply allow the vacuum of my aloneness, even loneliness, to be a source of revelation. Indeed, gracious surprises were here waiting to embrace me.

The most important relationship we can all have is the one you have with yourself, the most important journey you can take is the one of self-discovery. To know yourself, you must spend time with yourself, you must not be afraid to be alone. Knowing yourself is the beginning of wisdom. (Aristotle)

Wandering alone, deep in reflective thought, is more profound and elegant than what I encounter mystically and religiously. It is the bedrock of my intellectual integrity and emotional authenticity, for it has helped me to form the ideas and values that matter most to me. I suspect that many who read these words may share this enjoyment as well, that each of us enjoys our "time alone" and the insights flowing our way.

Alone on the Beach

Now, forever has come and gone. My body grows tired and pained with age, and slowly loosens its hold on my free spirit. I come to realize that our light can cast aside shadows, exposing our common humanity and beautiful differences, enrich us, fascinate us, even redeem us.

Freedom is what you do with what's been done to you. (Jean-Paul Sartre)

Gazing at my personal library, I reflect on the depth of intellectual rigor and contemplation laced in their pages. I also reflect at my own limited understanding of such ideas. The wisdom residing here is surpassed nearly every day in the reflections of ordinary people around me, who in simple words and shared feelings, *find heart*. Many of their experiences flow out of their "alone time."

Cherish your aloneness and its extraordinary gifts, ones that will expand with age.

Mere Color on Canvas

ॐ

Philosophy questions how and why
we become who and what we are
with much polemics and little certainty
a classic debate renewed
with the birth of each child

All are pieces of the same puzzle

Much in nature shapes us
genes, family, culture, universe
character, personality, preferences
biological and cultural determinism
spiced by stardust at our core

Deeper ignorance of hidden causes persists

Our hearts hear a different voice
intelligence, imagination
liberate us from nature's grasp
decisions freely flow from reason
self-awareness steers us forward

"There are no strings on me" (Pinocchio)

The universe argues for determinism
the human essence argues for free will

while truth rests in a blended being

caged by nature, liberated by mind

life's journey full of purpose and promise

Final truth is unsettling

We cannot expect finality

as so much is beyond us

we seek to rise above restraints

defeat denial, delusion

forge our tiny path forward

Fly away

In the artistry of creation

an artwork unfinished

an artist in embryo

canvass and colors of life

art falling short of dreams

Mere color on canvas

Relax

ৡ

Maybe relax in another lifetime
too many complications in this one
weighing heavily upon me
extenuating circumstances
dysfunctional relationships
compromised wellbeing
struggling to cope
seldom relaxing

My oldest daughter
invites me to join her
along the beach
at dawn's low tide
fog heavy around us
exquisite beauty
peaceful tranquility
hoping I might relax

My son is kind
suggests meditation
to relax, to let go
taking me on hikes
to submit mindfully
to the beauty of nature

reflective conversation

hoping I might relax

My youngest daughter

whispers her wisdom

kneels next to me

in her flower garden

in beauty beheld

in cherished memories

of love, healing

hoping I might relax

My grandchildren

invite play, laughter

full of life in the sun, rain

teach so much, so well

hug me wonderfully

lift me into their space

no rush, no worries

hoping I might relax

My wife is my muse

deeply sanguine

a butterfly in flight

spontaneity with sunshine

lifting me with dreams

her hand in mine

holding me close

hoping I might relax

Without them

I am an utter failure

so I write these words

on a restless night

doing something, anything

without a remote sense

of lasting peace

never ever relaxing

REVERENCES

Meditations

ॐ

Alone in my hammock in the forest near my home, I try to relax and let go of concerns bombarding my mind on this quiet summer afternoon. I try to let go of pain radiating out of my body. I have considered *meditation* in the past, but my efforts were mostly stuck in boredom and mindlessness, inventing mystical sentience at times. Meditation may be overrated, yet I admittedly practice it ineptly. On this day, I am ready to try again, patiently attempting to center my being in the natural world. I focus on the present, consciously suspending thoughts external to this moment. Not easy at first as it entails an act of sheer will and discipline, not relaxation and faith. I suspect meditation, like any form of art, takes skill and practice over time to master, if ever.

As I gaze up at the trees and sky, I am immersed in a sensual palette of color, shape, light, shadow, motion, sound, smell, and sensation. It beckons me to become part of its beauty and wonder. I try to relax and give in to it. Looking high above through a cluster of maple, oak, and fir trees surrounding me, I behold infinitely changing patterns of light and shadow, upon shades of greenery in exquisite variety. This swaying canopy of life beckons my imagination, inviting me to join in its magical dance. My breathing slows, my mind empties, and I am beheld by this sensual moment, sensing the quantum skips and pulses of my consciousness in relation to the natural world around me. I try not to think about what is happening to me, only to embrace it emotionally. Not easy.

I wander with a vagabond heart, drifting from color to shape to motion to the whispers of nature. Moving my vision up along the tree branches, one by one, my body stretches to join them in their reach to the sky. I admire the curvature of each branch, its separations into extended growth, its wounds from past storms, and its disappearance into the canopy of leaves above me. Time vanishes as I observe the minute details of nature, concentrating on them fully to admire their delicate intricacy. My presence expands its breadth and depth. I am relaxing more fully, breathing more deeply, sensing more completely. Leaves, needles, and blossoms invite me to reach out to them, be with them, become them. I marvel at the variegated shape of the revealed blue sky through the leaves, changing slowly with each breath of nature. Shapes and shades are unique, constantly shifting in the gentle breeze, migrating my mindlessness into mindfulness.

I hang on to color and shape for as long as it takes to fill my entire being, to allow it to draw me into its space, to inhale its sweetness, to listen to its song, to be present with all that is in this moment of existence. I feel my own face and honor its shape and texture, my own fingers and skin, my hair. I move within myself, rocked gently in my hammock by incoming wind from the west, still cool with ocean air. Here is energy, vibrating around me, within me, sustaining the miracle of life, my life. Scents of grass and flowers playfully greet me. The forest is so much older than I, reminding me of my youth and impermanence. It feels so good to be alive. To exist. To be. To become.

I hear faint calls of birds come and go, fleeting and enchanting. I see squirrels climb the tree branches, frolicking without haste. I imagine being one of them. I see hawks circling high above, joining in the art of all that is. I imagine flying with them. Raccoons are hiding in the brush nearby unmoved by my presence, as are the twin fawns hiding in the tall grass of meadow below, among the daisies. We all share this sacred place. I exhale distraction and nonsense from my mind and inhale only peace and clarity. Clouds flow by, revealed in small openings above. All in nature calls to me, moving gracefully in the same stream of spacetime in which I exist, forever present, inexplicably yet inseparably. A profound sense of reverence for living things implodes into my core being. My hammock rocks gently, and I drift off to near sleep, dreamless, taken far away, far within this moment.

The natural world heals deeply. It reaches out for our wounds, pain. It heals completely if we embrace it completely. The world, even the universe, is alive. It is alive beyond the presence of living creatures and plants. It resides indelibly and intimately in the fibers of my being. Whatever gives life in the span of cosmic existence also gives life to me in this moment. As I relax more fully, pain in my being dissipates, issues in the immediate foreground fade as I drift to higher ground. I am more whole, more alive, more one with the natural world.

As much as I hoped, I confess of never experiencing a sense of universal quantum consciousness, connecting me somehow with something much deeper in the fabric of our universe, even in the natural environment around me. The Buddha is smiling: mind and cosmos may be reaching out to me or emerging within me perhaps. I do not know. I am uncertain as to whether I can know. However, my doubts do not foreclose possibility.

I pull myself up into a more alert state and hours pass as minutes, the sun moves across the sky, the clouds thicken, the wind changes direction, blowing a light shower toward me, cooling my body. Rather than retreat, I allow it to touch me, merging with the earth, caught in the flow of nature, one with it. The grass drinks and the trees bathe. A freshness covers me, flows into me. I feel the moist, misty rain on my face, gently nourishing me. The shower passes quickly and widening streams of sunlight dry me, renew me. I am fully and wondrously alive. I breathe deeply, offering homage to life.

Before rising, I feel every part of my body, one by one, celebrating my living being. It is hard to move. I feel the peace in my being, even a reservoir of energy, sustaining me. I will seek another day to retreat to my hammock in the forest, to meditate again. To understand more fully what is, what I am. To not be concerned about why.

Nature's Gift

ৎ

Soon after moving to Oregon in 1974, we started looking for country property on which to build our future family home. We found a beautiful location close to town with a high elevation, wide western view, and a forest wilderness to the east. We purchased it, contingent upon a good water source. Given the expense of well digging, maybe the water spring marked with an "X" on the 1894 homestead map might be a source. We hiked up the east slope, and hidden among the ferns and trees, barely noticeable, was a pond of water about six feet in diameter and a foot deep. I took a water sample, had it tested, and discovered the water was pure.

A gift of nature.

The pressing question was how to develop this water source for our home use? Initially, it was difficult to estimate its flow and volume, much less its reliability. Having a strong back and weak bank reserves, I opted to dig out the spring in an effort to examine its hidden source and estimate its flow. I drained the pond and dug into the hillside for a few days, discovering a wide rock face under two towering old growth Douglas Fir trees. Water was flowing out of it in several spots, gently, steadily, about three gallons per minute. Marginal, perhaps, as acceptable wells yielded at least ten gallons per minute.

I contacted the State and County to determine if I could develop this water source. They granted water rights, but could not tell me how best to develop the water system. Time for creative thinking: "trap" the water in some manner, store it in a holding tank, and pipe it to my homesite. Over a three-month period in the summer of 1976, I dug out the hillside completely to reveal the rock face (water source), built a device to capture the water, installed pipes to transport it, and tested the system to determine its adequacy. It worked. The water was retested for quality, and the spring was certified as a water source. I sealed it with two tons of river rock, tarp, and soil—only a pipe from the spring was exposed above the earth. My young children have less than fond memories of hauling buckets of rock up the hill to the spring. We placed a large holding tank just below the site and installed overflow and outlet valves. Connecting the pipe to the tank, it filled completely within eight hours. Time for celebration! The overflow water was diverted to a large trough, so that animals who used the spring, would continue to have water. Concerned about the tank water freezing in the winter, a constant flow of water at the inside top of the tank was maintained to prevent such; it worked. It took nearly three weeks to dig a deep trench, downhill through rocks, roots, and clay, in which to lay water pipe to our homesite, connecting to a water pump and pressure tank in the pump room which I had yet to build. With water finally at the homesite, we could mix cement, and begin to lay the foundation for our home. No rest, as home construction was beginning on Labor Day, and winter rains start in late October.

Our home was built, and we celebrated again the day when we turned on the faucets to enjoy our spring water. After severe wind and ice storms over the next few years, the water tank was at risk of damage from fallen "widow-maker" limbs, large and heavy, from the towering fir trees. So dead branches were trimmed, generating added expense; home finishing projects had to wait for another year.

I never anticipated the spring would be a constant gift of nature to us for more than forty years. There were times when the water trap was compromised and had to be dug out and repaired, and the tank had to be repaired. The seasons rolled along. The spring kept flowing. Nature fills me with gratitude with each sip of pure spring water.

Life is much like our spring. It keeps flowing, steadily. It sustains us if we honor and protect it.

A gift of nature.

Black Walnut

৵

As I rest in my hammock on this quiet, summer afternoon, I am captivated. Towering above the maples and oak trees around me at my home in the Oregon countryside is an old black walnut tree, hundreds of feet high and over a hundred years old. It is majestic in size and presence. As I look up through the maples and oaks, I can see its highest branches, hundreds of them, stirring in the breeze with over a thousand delicate leaves. It fills an enormous space on the lower western slope of Spencer Butte.

As I drift into a dreamless space, the towering black walnut speaks to me. It is much older than I, and much wiser. It speaks of strength and restraint, of being both strong and gentle. It speaks of reaching to the sun, of allowing others to bask in its life-giving wonder. It speaks of the shadow it casts, hoping to shield and protect all beneath its reach. It speaks of life's trials, of the damage it has absorbed and of what it has learned. It is a sentinel in the natural world, adding to the beauty of the forest, and whispering of the beauty of life. There are days when I simply yearn to hike up near its huge trunk and look straight up as it spreads its many branches. I wonder what it has seen and heard, the stories it could tell.

A hard ice storm brought the old black walnut crashing to the earth. Its life was over. Its root system could not hold it any longer in its reach to the sky. It rested on the slope, broken with its many branches shattered. I hiked to its base, marveled at its presence, and hugged its trunk, weeping because my friend was gone. My conservative friends would smile at this old tree-hugging hippie, but think about it: a part of my sense of place was lost. And a part of my inner peace space was ripped away forever.

Its trunk and limbs were converted into lumber, used primarily for furniture. Its base and roots were used for tools. The small branches and leaves were cleaned up by my granddaughter and me. In the end, a silent tribute was offered and new seedlings were planted, hoping that one day, in a hundred years, one of them might fill the sacred place of my friend.

Bird Hunter

ॐ

On an autumn morning, we rise early and travel far, reaching our destination as the sun rises. Walking through the thick undergrowth of the forest, as quietly as possible, we search for quail. I am not with nature photographers, but hunters. Finally, in a clearing, one springs to the sky, and guns fire, blowing one wing off. It falls to the earth, and our dog quickly retrieves it. It is still alive and bleeding, so its throat is slit. My two companions cheer, raising their *kill* to the sky as a trophy of their sport. They look at me puzzled as to why my shotgun never fired? No words are spoken. I unload my gun, placing shells in my pocket, and strapping it to my back, as we move on in search of more trophies. Something is seriously wrong here! Nature has been violated!

I remain quiet. Philosophy sneaks up on me, causing me to ponder what just occurred. I wonder what delight is found in the terror we impose? Life is taken without conscience or even purpose. What rite of passage is served? How is our manhood magnified? What darkness is lurking in our evolutionary residue, our survival instincts, our need for dominion, our collective unconscious compelling us to take life from an innocent being? I find no cause for celebration, only for mourning the loss of life, and the loss of character in my friends. It is wrong of me to be here in the first place, caged in this alien ritual. Not having an exit route back to sensibility, I endure the "hunt," and the anguish swelling in me, inflicting just pain for my presence.

We walk out of the forest, passing a nest of quail chicks, crying for food. They will perish. Life is fragile in the forest. They are ignored, as we hike on, perhaps with their mother in our hunting bag. When I return home from my one and only hunting experience, I vow to never go hunting again. My two hunting partners become distant, as they fail to persuade me to overcome my disdain, and become a "real man."

Another day, I found myself in a forest, hiking a high mountain trail. There in a meadow filled with beautiful wildflowers, was a doe with two newborn fawns. She looked at me, frozen in terror, as our eyes met. I imagined for an instant being a hunter, wondering if I could pull a trigger to end her life. Just for sport! Just to affirm my manhood! I smiled, knowing that I never could. I stood motionless, as a feeling of profound reverence for life arose in me, respecting their presence on the earth. This sensation radiated across the meadow to her being as I approached her. She did not run. She continued to sit by her fawns in the high grass, as I passed within a few feet of her. Peace was heavy in the air. The sound of a distant hawk rang clear. I could feel the cool wind on the back of my neck, and her heartbeat in the center of my soul. From a ledge above, I could see her still, gazing up at me, as her fawns played around her. All in nature bound us together.

When my children were young, I prohibited them from playing with toy guns and in games of violent aggression. When children do, they teach adults much. With toy guns, they seldom hunt for game; rather, they hunt each other: human kill! When I was young, we played "Cowboys vs. Indians," and there was never any doubt as to who the bad guys were, and that they always died. We celebrated not just defeating, but killing the enemy as an act of American patriotism. Today, violent video gaming is arguably a community health problem. Even in the modern colosseum of aggressive spectator sports, violence is applauded more often than team performance. A serious flaw indeed in the character of humanity.

Violence deeply saddens me. It is woven into the fabric of our existence, into the shadows of our society. What concerns me is not just the violence bred of criminality or terrorism, but a force lurking much deeper in the barbaric residue of our evolved nature, nearly immune to ultimate expunge, inviting combat with living things, and in the end, an emotional outburst without provocation. Hunting provides an outlet for such violence, and to a lesser degree, so do most competitive sports. Our character is imprinted, even beyond our genetic endowment, by such activities. Watch adults hunt, and listen to their talk during and after such hunts. Watch children play with weapons or violent video games, and watch their mood shift and listen to their talk. How easy it is to pass the nest of those chicks, how easy to harden our hearts to what really matters. These rituals of violence ultimately transform us into the prey as we exterminate our humanity.

My naïve idealism envisions a meltdown of all weapons, and community rehabilitation for those who resist such. Only wishful thinking. I wonder if there is an abundance of intelligent life in the universe? If so, how likely is it that they would ever contact us? In their eyes, we are a risk. What if such a meltdown of weapons was contingent upon contact with other intelligent life in the universe?

As a child, my uncle lived with us when he returned from combat in WWII and the Korean War. His military ribbons and metals were impressive, but what was even more impressive was his firm insistence that I not play war games with toy soldiers and tanks. When he saw me playing other violent killing games with my friends, he would ask me to take a walk with him or play a card game. Whenever I asked him about the wars he fought, he became distant, and changed the subject, never talking about them.

Will we ever be capable of advancing our civilization, albeit our human nature, to live in peace? Not likely. Especially when we have gun raffles at local churches to raise funds to support extreme political causes. Especially when the most prosperous store in some small rural American towns is the gun store. Especially when we are incapable of enacting sensible gun control legislation. Will we ever wake up?

Into the Darkness

ॐ

On an early summer evening beneath a clear sky, alone, I wander high up the west slope of Spencer Butte into the darkening forest. I find much to behold, and I am beheld by much. In shafts of sunlight, there is vibrant color and revelation of the natural beauty, the unspeakable wonder of abundant life, and the boundless miracle of creation. The light draws my attention so fully that it is easy to ignore the shadows, to hike on by, for the darkness is cool and damp, filled perhaps with nasty, ugly things. Moving the sun off my face, I stop myself, turning into the darkness, moving to places untouched by light, nearly hidden and still. I feel the moist bark, smell the musky earth, and lift the ferns, branches, and logs to see what they might reveal. Here are surprises of nature that might otherwise be missed, finding a way to persist and sustain life. The more closely I explore the darkness, the more I am drawn to it, discovering beauty. The sun is touching the western horizon, and the darkness is deepening. I watch it close in around me, wondering what revelations await.

Pausing to sit on a fallen log, I have no sense of time, only a sense of the vast old-growth forest around me, teaching me. In my deepest awareness, I am both light and shadow, rejoicing in lightness and reflecting in darkness, these ancient interwoven fibers at the core of my being, connecting me with all that is. Without both light and darkness, I am philosophically anemic. If I pause too long, the sun will be gone, and the darkness of the forest will overwhelm me. Only my headlamp will lighten the trails back down the butte. I resist reaching for it, and instead, reach for my hammock and netting, roping it to trees, and crawling into my sleeping bag just in time as all light vanishes. I will spend the night up here, alone in the serene impenetrable darkness. Not even the moon or stars will likely touch me. Even my hand before my face cannot be seen. At first, I am immersed in absolute silence, but gradually, the forest comes alive, all around me. There are sounds of animals moving or wind in the trees. Unrecognizable sounds, too. There are fragrances of fir and pine. My hammock rocks in a gentle breeze. I see a narrow shaft of moonlight nearby, come and go. My initial anxiety dissipates into the peace of the forest, a forest that is much older than I, alive and growing, on the skin of this distant, tiny planet at the edge of our galaxy. Our universe is mostly darkness, but not empty, as there is something (supposedly dark matter and energy) in the darkness, too. And there is something wondrous here that exists in the darkness, and I am discovering its grace. Reverence holds my deepest being, so profound and promising in its haunting embrace.

The complications of life can consume light and create darkness. One of my students was overwhelmed with complications in his senior college year: cancer, a pregnant girlfriend, few financial resources, a heavy academic load, and dwindling job prospects. He considered dropping out of school. His darkness was deep, indeed. With a bit of encouragement and a lot of his own resolve, he accepted a meager job opportunity, learned from it, and eventually converted it into not only a successful business but an incredible life. He did not run out of the darkness, rather he embraced it fully, and discovered the light he chose to bring into his life. Now, he uses his resources to help others in their journeys.

Rubbing my philosopher's stone, I seek not just better answers to better questions, but insight from the endless flow of questions about questions. I muse that questions are ultimately better than answers in enriching our being. I wonder about virtue and vice, given humanity's propensity for good and evil. Both are pervasive in the human condition. It is not surprising that our art, literature, and religion pay homage to light, admonishing us to seek and embrace it because goodness and truth flow from it. Conversely, darkness should be avoided, even feared because it is empty or maybe evil.

My thoughts focus on a friend who has been battling cancer for nearly two decades, with quiet patience and resolve to endure suffering, so the hope of a new day is fulfilled. We mostly encounter her in the light of optimism and recovery, but there are times when a few of us join her in the darkness when hope and resources fade. It is there that my friend finds her strength is resilient and true, even greater than ours. She has little fear of the darkness for she refuses to deny it as part of her. Her faith sustains her, not merely in religion, but in her personal eternity.

The virtue of patience arises most often in darkness, when life is full of ugly complications, when conflict or ill health or death is upon us. Only because of the discipline of patience do I discover things. Patience entails listening to others closely, to suspend my own preoccupations, to give in to the flow of being in another, to seek understanding first before trying to be understood. In the shadows of life, patience leads us to feel what others are feeling, to look beyond the words of easy discourse, to empathize with the pain of suffering and grieving, not to share it so much as to embrace it together. I do not fully know what compassion is, but I know it requires patience, a willingness to move into the shadows and embrace pain and agony, at the core of our being. Virtue is free to flourish in this state of being, to cage and quiet vice. In the shadows, I come to embrace the pain of poverty, disease, starvation, mental illness, death, and injustice. The presence of such evil in the world serves no noble purpose, with or without God to hold our hand. Suffering with another person, in their hour of darkness, is redeeming for all who share such pain.

A person in our greater family suffered a brain aneurysm that nearly took her life in her prime. In the light of day, there were positive thoughts and energy, providing comfort and promise. In the shadows, however, helplessness and unspoken suffering stung deeply. Fighting for proper treatment and care, it took strength born in the shadows, not the light, to prevent the universe from having its way. I do not know if there is a God or not, nor do I pretend to know how the universe works. What I do know is this: life is precious. We need to cling to it for as long as possible; we need to combat injustice and death with all of our strength. What matters most may ultimately succumb to what matters least. Coping with suffering and injustice in the shadows of life, we go on and refuse to give in.

Morning comes quickly, as birds start singing with the faintest trace of sunrise. The darkness is lifting, as sunlight begins to penetrate the forest. I am well rested, having slept in my cradle of darkness. I awoke several times during the night by the sounds of the forest, seldom fearful. Dreams seem deeper, richer, out here. The darkness around me held much, just as the darkness within me may hold much. My body stretches fully, not too eager to leave the hammock. I survey the canopy of life high above me and even feel a brief morning shower on my face. It seems so good to be a living miracle. As the forest brightens out of darkness, I enter the metaphor that we brighten out of our darkness, too. Our quiet resilience sustains us, unnoticed.

As a teacher, I have seen both light and darkness in the faces of my students. All are endowed with bright minds and beautiful spirits. Some never wander into the darkness, and never learn its many lessons. Most have an abundance of both, moving in and out of the shadows. A few wander into the shadows and become lost in darkness, struggling to cope with life's burdens and demons. Mustering the resources of the university and family to intervene, tragedy was mostly averted, with love and understanding. Not always, however. My heart aches with loss. I have seen its impact on family and friends. It is unwise to simply shower light into darkness, as it eventually fades. Rather, it is best to embrace the darkness, to learn from it (the reasons underlying dark impulses), and to address what we discover, before seeking light. Otherwise, we may only delay and not resolve critical issues. I take a breath for insight. I enjoy the hugs of former students who found their way back.

I lost a dear friend recently to cancer. His cancer was discovered several weeks prior to his death. He was a kind and beautiful man. I raged at the universe, but was reminded of his grace, and found serenity in his words:

I am that I am
I need no justification for my existence
I need no justification for any part of my existence
I need no justification for any act
I am that I am and no other reason

I am part of the nameless God

I am a stranger

I worship no thing

I worship that which language cannot reach

But must always attempt

I worship the God of history

The God that intervenes in human history

Through human nature

When I want to see an image of God

I look at another person

I am a human being

I am a man

I am a stranger

I am becoming what I have not been

I do not know what I will be

That is in God's hands

I only know that I will not be what I have been

I am a process not a thing

The thread of that process is my spirit

The thread is slack and allows me

Great wanderings from side to side on my journey

(Jon Garlinghouse, October 1988)

Rubbing my philosopher's stone harder, I remind myself that life's complications are not the only force that shuts out light and casts shadows, but our sheer ignorance also draws us into darkness. There is much we simply don't know, even though we may believe we know it. It may be well beyond the epistemological reach of our best science. The universe is far stranger and more peculiar than we imagine or even can imagine. Even with the pressing realities of life, knowledge may elude us, especially when our ignorance deceives us. The darkness is deep around us, indeed. As foreboding as this prospect seems, the unknown need not be daunting. When embraced, it is humbling. I delight in the mystery of it all, celebrate the surprises of discovery (and recovery), and find cause for faith in life. There is peace within me.

I rise and hike down the butte to my home. My dog leads the way. I sense that all in nature has been our companion in the light and shadow of the forest. I long to share my experience, but my family is away. No sound of laughter or conflict. No work or play either. The silence of the forest has followed me home. I drink my fresh spring water first, renewing me. I turn and slowly look back up the hill, marveling at the play of light and shadow, and the beauty of nature revealing itself to me as a parting tribute to our time together. I smile, knowing finally.

My Son's Life

ॐ

My son's life is
a path less traveled
finding his way alone
embracing wonder, grace
discovering his humanity

Not an easy life
running against the wind
resisting values others made
not kneeling to the wrong god
not missing his star, his life

His days are mostly uncertain
freedom laced with ambivalence
solitude deepened with reverence
rivers, mountains sweep him away
a spirit untamed, wild, free

His philosophy is uncluttered
more questions, fewer answers
his spirit wanders far
his imagination farther
among the stars at night

Mistakes were made

along his journey

age brings wisdom

leads to higher ground

peace in the morning sun

Out Here

৪৪

Only an old philosopher walks in hard rain that pounds on his shoulders like a heavy mountaineering pack. My walking is actually hiking, given the distance and terrain covered. I wander along the beach on the northern Oregon coast in the cold of winter, in the fury of nature. Strong wind, too, lifting the surf's spray into my face at times, as the surf rises and drives toward shore, surprising me at high tide.

I am the only person out here. *A bit crazy perhaps.*

So, alone, nearly extinct, except for fleeting thoughts, reflective ones, giving warmth when the chill finds me. The sky, so dark and foreboding, sinks into me.

Why am I here? I smile at the reply rising out of my being like the surf sweeps toward shore. I am here because I am *drawn.* By the ocean, surf, beach, wind, rain, clouds, sky, and a few birds who sense this call to life.

Here is only the interplay of being and nature, an inexplicably haunting embrace, beheld in this exquisite moment. No media distractions out here, no bizarre politics, no radical religious voices, no lurking economic terrorism, no ugly social turmoil, no gods or demons either. All are uninvited, repelled by this place. They flow out of my mind like the wind off my back, as silent meditations engage me with each stride.

The rain and wind ease, and I stop to take a long, deep breath, spreading my arms upward to pay homage to all that is. I discover that the incoming surf has cut off the beach to the north and south, isolating me in front of high cliffs. I have been in this situation before, sparking adrenaline in my bloodstream, challenging an aging body. My options are few. Find a high spot on the rocks and wait for a few hours. Or, climb up a steep, muddy slope of hemlock and spruce to higher ground. Sensing the tide is becoming stronger, I opt to climb out, in mud over my boots and in thick, tangled undergrowth. As the climb steepens, the rain and wind pick up to affirm my mortality.

North Beach

I am the only person out here. *A bit crazy for sure.*

Memories flow from my depths, learnings of having previously been in this very predicament. No fear. No rush. No tomorrow or yesterday. Immediate presence is all I am. Sitting on a high ledge, the beach is in fog below me and I hear only the strong surf crashing into the rocks. I imagine being swept out to disappear in the darkness. Not today. Instead, I take another long breath and imagine a tamer beach with my children and their children laughing in a warm sun and playing in an easy surf. I smile and wipe the rain and tears from my face.

Climbing higher, I find a narrow deer trail and hike south through the dense old growth coastal forest, contending with steeply uneven terrain filled with downed trees and flash flooding streams. I head home, though it seems like a mere resting place. The beach is my home, the place where my spirit lives, calling me, calling me back.

Grand Canyon Tribute

ॐ

There are "mountains to climb and rivers to run" has been a melodic theme arising from the depths of my being for most of my life. The wilderness seems to speak to me in different ways, at different times, for different reasons, with different effects. There, I discover my purest imagery, deepest freedom, and truest self. It invites an endearing romance with the earth itself, full of surprising discoveries and intriguing mysteries. My experiences and reflections in the Grand Canyon are one such romantic encounter. I seek to preserve these cherished memories before they fade forever, so that my family and friends may be inspired to go there someday.

Getting There: Only twenty pounds in my backpack, the bare essentials to survive, I have little to slow me down. Flying just above the canyon in a small plane, dropping at times below the rim, I am overwhelmed by the grandeur and enormity of this place, beheld in its embrace. The pilot drops me off near a small lodge on the north rim, alone. Refusing to allow nature to play to an empty house, I enjoy a breath-taking sunset before sleep beckons. It comes easy as I dream of the adventure ahead, and ignore the bugs and spiders crawling all over me at night.

Day One: A dark sky with distant thunder and lightning awakens me in the early morning. Putting our rafts in the water near Lees Ferry, the wind chill drops to twenty degrees. The promise of the canyon's splendor along with the insulation of my life jacket keeps me warm. Heading downstream as the hard rain and wind hit with dismal force, I sit at the front of our raft, alone mostly, not wanting to miss what nature is unfolding before me. My toes are blue, and my hands are numb. The incredible wilderness is closing in around me, in me.

After seven hours on the Colorado, at times with unclear separation between river and sky, we set up camp early near Vasey's Paradise, just past Stanton's Cave. Narrow, side canyon streams have swollen and there is risk of flash flooding, posing a life-threatening risk to hikers. Our guide tells stories of hikers disappearing without a trace under such conditions. The walls of Marble Canyon rise steeply around me, and cascading sunlight off the canyon walls in bright red, orange and yellow hues, offer hope for a better tomorrow. Hiking down the river, I leave the friendly chatter of the campfire behind. Life abounds gracefully around me: A black duck and three tiny ducklings float by; wrens dart through the thick brush, skipping on the river's surface; two bighorn sheep transcend the steep canyon wall across from me; a red-spotted toad sits on a nearby rock and ponders my alien presence; and a pair of bald eagles circle high above, nesting on the canyon wall. Spacetime curves to this point and place, focusing my senses. I no longer *behold* the wilderness around me; rather, I am *beheld* by it. The universe is suddenly more magical than mysterious, less existentially unfriendly and foreboding, creating *a slight crack in the cosmic egg*, even a brief tear in the fabric of reality, shifting from a peak to a *peek* cognition, revealed here in the wilderness alone. Just maybe life is not a mere perchance, but something more wondrous transcends our naive sense of reality, something subtle and surprising, unseen and unheard, but known within, completely inarticulate, not just in my being alone, but in all that is. It stirs an awakening of a much deeper part of existence, less discovery than *re*covery, less cognition than *re*cognition. There is incredible peace in moments such as these, and a yearning to fill my life with them. This old skeptic is in awe. My hands and toes are warm again.

Day Two: Just down river from camp, we stop at a large natural amphitheater, Redwall Cavern. John Wesley Powell wrote in his journal that it could hold 5000 people. Maybe 500 at best! All river runners tend to exaggerate. The wilderness seems to forgive these excesses in our stories, as our imagination is so magnified here. Our conscience is magnified, too. It reveals a clear voice: preserve our rivers and their ecosystems and dismantle more dams. Edward Abbey haunts me again. Preserve ancient cultures, too. Several caves along the way have figurines cached under rock cairns by natives of the Desert Culture, dating back 3000 years. One can feel their spirit. Just past Nankoweap Rapid, 500 feet above on the canyon wall, are Anasazi granaries (small caves). Good climbers, these Anasazi. Their harvests were protected in such high places, free of moisture and rodents.

The narrow slice of grey sky high above the canyon clears into a bright blue, and all offer loud praise to the sun. Long hours on the river, no serious rapids yet, I float mostly in my kayak, relaxing, taking it all in with unbroken silence. Red-tailed hawks circle high overhead. A ringtail cat, unique to the canyon and smart as a raccoon, wanders by.

Along a wide, panoramic bend in the river with towering canyon walls, we set up camp at a lush, green oasis with a wide, sandy beach. Tamarisk grows everywhere, waving in the wind. An Arizona Sister (butterfly) floats by gracefully. A reddish Helleborine orchid plant is blossoming next to me. A canyon tree frog stares hard at me. Noticing rainbow trout as the sun exposes the river bottom, I go for an early evening swim, floating downstream in the strong current for a half mile. Cold water cleanses and refreshes my weary body, but most question my sanity. A Great Blue Heron stands motionless in the river as I float close by. I hike back to camp past flowering hedgehog, barrel, and fishhook cacti. Ocotillo reaches through the tall grass to show its bright, red splendor. I sit on a high ledge for over an hour in complete stillness, inhaling it all with each breath, basking in the peace of this place. Sleep comes easy outside my tent tonight, caressed by the cool river breeze. I am not alone. The whole universe is my companion.

Day Three: During the night, I awake and am beheld by the stars. Even the still river eddies reflect the heavens above. I am beheld by the cosmos. Lying on my back on the sand, I imagine the earth rotating beneath me. The sound of the river lifts me skyward, and I float into the Milky Way. The canyon whispers that life always finds a way to survive, adapt, and evolve into something stronger, in this harsh environment. As I gaze upward. I wonder, in this vast universe, if life finds a way to persist, somehow, somewhere out there. And if life on this planet can evolve in such dazzling diversity and resiliency, would it not be reasonable to assume that the universe is filled with an abundance (and diversity) of life far greater than we can imagine? Just maybe, we are not alone, only separated by our primitive ignorance.

Morning brings a perfect day! At the confluence of the Little Colorado, we hike upstream as the water turns turquoise and warm, and float down through small rapids and narrow chutes. Later, above Unkar Rapid, I swim across the river with our guide and hike up to an ancient Indian ceremonial site. Finding a metate and a mano (Anasazi stones) used to mill corn, it prompts reflection on what life was like to live under such conditions. Hardship is a relative state of mind, it seems, without a reference point. I wonder if I could have done it and still had moments to capture the essence of life. Some passing Anasazi spirits are smiling with me, perhaps. Later, we approach the Inner Gorge and set up camp above Sockdolager Rapid. Exhausted! Just killed a bark scorpion nearby, the first one I've seen. It stung me on the foot, and later I become a bit sick. Glad the red ants are diurnal. Spiders aren't; they seem bigger down here, especially when they crawl on you at night. Need to rest well, as this old body seems eager to keep up with my younger adventurous spirit.

Day Four: At dawn, we enter the Inner Gorge. The surprising variety of geological formations, spanning millions of years reveal layers of schist, limestone, shale, quartzite, and sandstone. Looking at the pure mass of this place, a sense of awe speaks of my own minuteness in the total scheme of things. I have to pull myself out of my meditative space, as major rapids come fast: Bright Angel, Granite, Hermit, and infamous Crystal. Big white water, fast, long, dropping sharply among big boulders as the river snakes through the narrow canyon. No space for misjudgment here. Stopping to recover from exhaustion, we hike a mile up a narrow canyon with a beautiful, turquoise stream, past small waterfalls, tall cottonwood trees, and blossoming purple phacelia and cardinal monkey-flowers. On a few vertical rock ledges are yellow flowering prickly-pears. Beauty. Finding a warm swimming hole, I stay for nearly an hour. My spirit is connecting with this place, seeping into it. Perhaps, the inner landscape at the core of my being is similar to the canyon, ancient, rugged, and omniscient. Hiking to camp, I bathe in the very cold Colorado. My hair is clean, blowing in all directions, resembling a barrel cactus. I laugh out loud at myself, sensing my spirit is at home here.

In the late afternoon, we set up camp. I pitch my tent on a high ridge 300 feet above the river to gain a tremendous view and to capture more wind and shade. Everyone below will remain in the sun for another two hours. I inhale spiritual nourishment from each breath, closing my eyes to listen to the canyon's song. I imagine having wings and gliding down the canyon as I meditate. The steady breeze lifts me skyward. My eyes open to a more vivid world filled with the exquisite wonders of life, a magical world whose essence is coupled with mine in ways too infrequently sensed. Lying on my back, I watch hawks circling 300 feet above me and feel the wind under my wings. Reincarnation haunts me. I marvel at rock overhangs suspended against the law of gravity, ready to break loose and fall on this exact spot, crushing me, yet photos of these exact walls some fifty years ago reveal little change.

Our lifetime is so short compared to the age of this place. Again, the river current whispers that my being is as ancient as the canyon itself.

Day Five: Restless, much to my good fortune, I got up about 3 AM with the canyon walls dark and the sky star-filled, but suddenly the 2000-foot canyon wall downriver to the west *literally lit up*, becoming totally luminous, as did the river itself. *Celestial vaulting* is an extraordinary natural phenomenon. Apparently, the full moon was low on the horizon to the southeast behind me, not visible and its light reflected off the canyon wall, creating a powerful stream of light entering the dark canyon below it. Surreal. I was too stunned to move but eventually drifted back to sleep.

Mornings are always early on the river, as we prepare to enter the narrowest and darkest part of the Inner Gorge. We run several challenging rapids, slamming into a rock wall in one and nearly flip our raft in fast, big white water. Later, we stop for two hikes. The first one is only a half mile up an extremely narrow, side canyon whose walls can be touched on both sides as a person stands in the middle, yet they rise several hundred feet above us. The limited light reflects red and orange hues, revealing sea life and plant fossils embedded in the rocks. Our guide points to one layer of rock, the "Great Unconformity" in which 200 million years of geological history is missing and for which scientists have no plausible explanation. Mysteries abound here. This canyon is filled with them. They lurk behind each bend in the river or side canyon, waiting to surprise our wandering spirit, to jolt us out of bounded rationality and tight emotionality. It is hard to imagine that this canyon was not created by the power of the Colorado cutting through its plain, but by the plain rising under the river, heaved up by forces under the crust of the earth. Even when mystery fades and science prevails in offering rational explanations, comprehension is difficult, much to creationists' delight and folly. Nature's way entices our imagination, and in the end, roots our being in the earth.

Later, we stop at Deer Creek, location of a tall waterfall close to the river's edge. Cooling off in its pool, a few of us prepare for a half-day hike, climbing up the canyon wall next to the falls, the Inner Gorge about 300 feet below. We enter the narrow side canyon from which the waterfall streams, climb along a narrow ledge with the stream 100 feet below and the canyon walls about forty feet apart, rising very high above us. Only a slim shaft of sunlight peaks through. Shadows are dark and thick. Our footing is unsteady because of loose rocks and uneven ledges. Of all of our hikes, this one raises my heart rate the most because of sheer vertical exposure, thus requiring a tremendous amount of concentration, patience, and strength. Along the traverse, I look up, noticing small handprints on the rock, left by Anasazi about 600 AD. I place my hand on one, inviting their spirit to speak to me, assuring me that the rock is stable and that they had stood on the same exact ledge as I. Hiking on, I discover a clear pool in a narrow band of sunlight, above tall twin falls, and surrounded by cottonwood trees, some nested by American Dippers. Chuckwalla are on the rock walls around us. We muse about the canyon's mysteries and wonders, and our guide speaks of Anasazi folklore and customs. Humility in the presence of natural wonder flows in my bloodstream. After a few hours, we hike out, invigorated, renewed.

A mystic is at home in the wilderness. A philosopher, too! Good companions, these two. The vast canopy of stars in the clear, desert sky, the unbroken solace and boundless wonder, the haunting desolation and grandeur of the canyon, the surprisingly lush greenery and abundant life, the quiet power and melodic sound of the river, the intricate interplay of sun and shadow, and much more holds our fragile life in its grasp. The wondrous artistry of it all and its mystical infusion into our being transforms us into something reborn, redeemed, and whole again. Somehow, I connect with each grain of sand, each cottonwood leaf, each drop of river water, each sound in the desert air, each color in its landscape, each star in the night sky. The wilderness, I discover, is at the core of my being. If any small element of this place is disturbed, an unsettled tremor in my being arises. There is so much more to this place, to this state of being, than I can hope to ever imagine. Drifting into mystical space, one disbelieves nothing and embraces everything. Naive metaphysics implode quietly. One only listens and openly invites the rush of ever-widening phenomenological engagement, drinking in nature's pure flow, its persistent, inarticulate, indelible revelation of what is. Known to us alone, in a way unknown and unfathomed.

We camp in a large grotto under an overhang, sheltered from sun and blowing sand while spotted sandpipers play along the river and pallid bats fly around us. I take a long, moonlight swim to cool off.

Days are getting longer and the nights shorter. The canyon walls seem to be higher and narrower. The wilderness is bending spacetime again. My senses are inseparable with nature around me. A part of my being will remain here forever. And a part of this canyon will reside in my being forever.

Surveying the Canyon

Day Six: There are clearly two worlds on this planet: the urban one out there and the one here in the wilderness. One embraces change and one is changeless. One congests the mind and spirit, and one liberates and invites flight. What is lost out there is replenished here. Out there, life is mostly on the circumference of being; here, we discover and authenticate our core. In this place, there is little distraction, only the flow of realization into what matters most.

Early in the day, we stop at Havasu Falls. We hike up the side canyon along a very narrow trail with unnerving vertical exposure. Below is a clear, turquoise blue stream with a series of small waterfalls and deep pools below them. Dragonflies and damselflies are abundant. Too many lizards to even begin to identify are blended into the desert landscape. A Grand Canyon rattlesnake basks in the sun on a nearby rock outcropping. White-tailed antelope squirrels play in the cottonwood trees. Nearing the deepest pool, I dive in and swim along the bottom as several large, brook trout swim by gracefully. Watching their smooth, effortless motion, I am drawn into a spell, and I mimic their rhythm, swimming with them. My breath lasts forever. I imagine being one of them. Free. Strong. Alone. Later, around a tight bend with steep walls, bighorn sheep graze next to the water with newborns hidden behind the rocks, briefly exposing themselves. They lift their heads in peace with our presence. It is unbelievable they survive here. Life goes on.

In the late afternoon, we approach Lava Falls, arguably the most dangerous rapid on the Colorado. We scout it to assess its shape, rocks, walls, and holes, and to discuss how best to run it under different water levels. Viewing it is a cause for fear. Rafts disappear here. People die here. It has one of the greatest drops and longest runs of any navigable rapid in the world. The time has come, though others in our party choose to hike around it. Entering the rapid, a tremendous wall of water crashes over the entire raft, pinning our backs to the equipment rack. Deep breaths as we are submerged in foam most of the time. Time stands still so I can fully experience the slowest minute of my entire life. The river, fast and powerful, has us in its grip. A nightmare for some, but a dream for me, beheld by the sheer size and terror of Lava Falls. It is hard to quiet my soul, but as night comes, the stars hold me again. Peace returns slowly to my being.

Day Seven: Morning comes early as we raft downriver to a helicopter landing spot. As our small helicopter lifts skyward, and the canyon gorge fades beneath me, my heart sinks. I imagine being a river guide and living here every summer. My spirit soars at the thought, albeit unrealistic. As the Grand Canyon fades on the horizon, I am drawn inward. The wilderness reaches out to me. I behold the canyon in my mind, pure, still, natural, and ultimately and intimately miraculous, *reflecting my own inner landscape*, full of color and wonder and mystery, a center to my being uncluttered by unnatural artifact and social custom, reaching for what is best in my relatively short existence. Just as life finds a way in the canyon, a profound reverence finds a way to emerge, to cause me to be more alive and vibrant.

We have run one of America's great rivers through one of the world's natural wonders for 183 miles, dropping in elevation over 2000 feet, and navigating 98 rapids. We have hiked side canyons, traversed steep canyon walls, swam in clear streams and the pools of beautiful waterfalls, studied geological formations and Native American cultures, enjoyed wondrous animal and plant life, and embraced the universe at night. When the wilderness enters the deepest strata of my being, and I feel the quiet pulse of its presence, smiling, I know there are even more "mountains to climb and rivers to run."

Note: Excerpts from my journal (June 1999). Only twenty percent of the content is provided in this essay, deleting much detail about rapids, hiking, and campsite conversations, focusing primarily on my experience of the natural environment.

Just Notice A Little Bit More

ॐ

Just notice a little bit more.

Notice the extraordinary in the ordinary, the mystical in the natural, and one may touch what is truly sacred. Notice the ordinary in the extraordinary, the natural in the unnatural, and one may discover enduring faith in life. Notice the mysterious dance in our unfolding being.

Notice the simple in the complex, the profound in what confounds, and one may embrace benevolent reverence. Notice the complex in the simple, what confounds the profound, and one may invite humility. Notice the echoes in the depths of consciousness.

Notice a little bit more. Every moment. It slips by quickly. We miss so much. Existence surrounds us, invites us, and entices us to notice all that is real and is possible. Notice that even the dark walls of Plato's cave reflect light, brightening each moment of our existence.

Notice the beautiful in the ugly, the goodness in the bad, the truth in the falsehood, and one may grasp the meaningful. Notice the ugly in the beautiful, the bad in good, the falsehood in truth, and one may develop empathy and compassion. Notice the rhythm of our being becoming more apparent as we experience life fully.

Notice the philosophical in the scientific, the poetic in the analytic, the mystery in the reality, and one becomes authentically human. Notice the divine in the human, the unknown in the known, the stardust in our being, and we invite wonder and beauty in our heart. Notice how we touch and love others.

Noticing a little bit more changes us. As we become beheld by love, reverence, humility, empathy, authenticity, wonder, mystery, and meaningfulness in the things we notice, we are lifted into a philosophically reflective life, connecting us intimately with all that is and has been. Notice that we realize how to live a life that matters.

We drift along this stream of fleeting existence, beheld in the current of time, turning over stones along the shore, seeing much more than imagined, and becoming much more than imagined, only if we just notice a little bit more.

Every Breath is a Prayer

ॐ

The morning sun barely hints of rising over the Annapurna to the east, under a thin crescent moon and a narrow dark, star-filled sky, framed by other high ridges to the west. Scorpio is still glowing to the south with its curved tail, last seen on a sailing vessel in the Virgin Islands decades ago. I am fully awake in this moment, as a cool breeze lifts me from my sleep, holds me in this exquisite moment. Every breath is a prayer. As the predawn haze begins to lift, the pink silhouette of sacred Machapuchare towers nearly 7000 meters, holding the promise of a new day of trekking the Nepali landscape. Hard cots and cold showers are quickly forgotten as the stunning white Himalayan massif reveals itself in the morning sun.

Hiking through thick forests of tall Rhododendron trees, bright blossoms are abundant and breathtaking. Colorful birds and butterflies are everywhere. The immense undergrowth contains even more gifts of beauty. The forests seem nearly endless in their expanse. Once above the forests, we hike upward and at times downward, to advance into the mountains. Reaching glaciers, we climb upward to high ridges where we see an endless flow of mountains on the horizon. Here, I can hold the rising and setting sun in the palms of my hands. Another truly mystical experience of grandeur and awe to behold.

At the end of the third week, we return to a small village below, to relax and rest. Curious, I wander around the village by myself, checking out street vendors and markets, watching the Nepali people as they find reason for gleeful exchanges in spite of their stark poverty in this incredibly harsh environment. In the distance, I hear the laughter of children, and I am drawn to a school with a teacher in the midst of an English lesson. "Hello" and "May I sit in" are returned with a smile and a gesture waving me in. The young children, faces glowing with precious smiles, are enchanted by my presence, as I am enchanted with theirs. The teacher asks them to greet me in English, and they do barely as their exuberance and laughter erupt. We exchange simple phrases in English, translated by the teacher, after which the children repeat my words, and I repeat their words in Nepalese. A bell rings to end school, and the children swarm around me as we walk back through the village. They laugh at the sound of the yak bell on my pack, a sound that they usually recognize as a yak in need of containment, but now simply point and refer to me as "a lost yak." The vibrancy of these beautiful children is so robust, nourishing my tired body, in the pure mountain air.

As the children begin to disperse, a small boy (age eight) and his even smaller sister take my hands pulling me up the mountain slope. The teacher is amused and indicates that they want to show me off to their parents. Nearly a mile later, we approach a small stone hut with a roof of limbs. A trail of smoke rises from a hole in the flat roof. The children rush in and pull their mother out; with anxious eyes she greets this foreign stranger. Gradually, a smile comes to her face, prompted no doubt by the gleeful playfulness of her children in my presence. She motions up the hill. In English, the boy says, "Father," whom they want me to meet.

Hiking up the slope, I am amazed by the terraced farmland, framed by narrow curving sections, stacked continuously upon a very steep slope, supported by hand-laid rock walls. After a short hike, we encounter a man kneeling in the dirt, attempting to repair his plow, a plow with an iron blade and a broken wooden frame. He rises to greet me with a smile, though his face masks despair. His children explain my presence, and he expresses gratitude to me for walking them home. His kind welcome bridges our cultures. I walk toward his plow and with facial and hand gestures, ask if I can help. He shakes his head in disgust, kicking the plow, no doubt profanely. He is surprised when I kneel in the dirt to inspect it, attempting to understand how it works. Several wooden joints are broken, and his spirit is further broken, at a loss as to how to repair it. It is his only plow, and it reflects considerable age and wear. I reach into my pack, remove a long length of nylon rope, immune to water and ice, cut it in sections, and then proceed to repair each of the broken joints, wrapped with self-tightening knots. Rising, I slap the yak, push the plow, and plow the ground to test it. It is tight and secure. I turn to see the man weeping, hugging his children close, his daughter in his arms, wiping his tears away. He lowers his children to the ground, and then embraces me, now crying profusely. His children join us.

This is my question: What really matters in life? It is inspiring to stand on high mountain ridges, to behold the incredible vistas. It is exquisite to wander through forests with their blooms, birds, and butterflies touching me with color and fragrance. Even so, I would not trade those moments for the one with this family high above that small village in Nepal. I muse that the most amazing gifts of nature are overwhelmed by purely intimate human kinship. They are deeper and eternal, lingering lastly in our setting sun.

As I hike under a dark, star-filled sky toward the village below, my every breath is a silent prayer to an unknown god: bless them, bless them.

Reflections on Infinite Shore

ॐ

**Many have walked before
along this isolated beach, some**

Our isolated home is this earth, this tiny speck in a vast universe, where our life emerges and ends. We wonder why? Are we more than imagined?

with carefree spontaneity, others

Some of us go through life, living, laughing, crying, working, learning as we go, without much philosophical reflection beyond the immediate concerns of life and survival.

with hurried desperation, each

Some of us are compelled to ensure our survival and prosperity, consumed by immediate life concerns, with only fleeting reflections of purpose and promise.

building their castles

We construct our lives, pursuing our education and professions, having our families, building our homes, and amassing our property and wealth.

dreaming their dreams

We may reflect on our lives. In widely different ways, we dream about our life journey. We dream about doing more, having more, being more. We may even dream about doing and having less. We become our dreams.

leaving their footprints
in the sand

Our life has an impact on others, for good or bad. Our life matters or not. We may influence others to be more, to be good, to combat evil, to embrace life, and to reach further.

All disappear, washed away

We all die and fade away. It is simply the way it is, no less, no more. Maybe.

by the outgoing tide, yet beheld,

We sense, rightly or wrongly, that as we "behold" the beauty and wonders of existence, we are "beheld" by them in some exquisitely haunting manner.

drifting upon the ocean's surface,

Our life after death continues to influence others for a while, and parts of us are evident in the character and personality of loved ones.

glimmering in the setting sun, and

The lives of the people we have touched for good will continue to "glimmer" with goodness and beauty.

in the beckoning darkness, rising

Those lives will touch others for good, an unspoken legacy of wisdom and virtue, as life moves forward, maybe sustained, maybe not.

as stars with infinite variety, wonder
in the clear, night sky

We are stardust. We return to this incredible mystery around us. We hope we are more than imagined. Maybe, maybe not. Those who honor us, look to the stars and wonder.

Note: The bolded poem is entitled Infinite Shore, *Finding Heart* (p.176).

Into Mountain Air

ॐ

Heading due south over 5,000 miles: Portland to Los Angeles to Lima to Cusco, my final destination is Machu Picchu, the "Lost City of the Incas," located high in the foothills of the Peruvian Andes. I plan to acclimatize and enjoy the culture of Cusco for two days then hike four "hard" days on the Inca Trail (82km) to the citadel of the ancient Inca Civilization in the fifteenth century.

The trail's landscape is covered by dense rainforests along the stunning snowcapped Andes mountains, with some peaks rising over 20,000 feet. These mountains are sacred to the Incas. While Machu Picchu sets at 8,000 feet, the trail's high point is 13,860 feet at Dead Woman's Pass. Around every turn and over every pass, incredible natural beauty awaits me.

Nature breaks its sunny promises, and hard rain comes at us, weighing us down. Arriving at the base of Machu Picchu four days later, everything I have, on me and in my pack, is rain-soaked. I smell really bad. I am exhausted. A hot shower and bed in a small hotel become my spiritual experience. The next morning, refreshed and dry, we hike up through the forest to the entrance of the lost city. As the thick mist lifts, the sun reveals one of the most breathtaking sights in the entire world. I am embraced by its presence. We hike southeast and climb the 10,000-foot mountain towering above it. From the summit, the view is of the snowcapped Andes massif, surging waterfalls adding to headwaters of the Amazon River, the immense Amazon jungle endlessly spreading eastward, and to the west below us, Machu Picchu.

The incredible natural landscape around me gives way to the equally wondrous architecture of this lost place. Laced into the fabric of this place is a mystery. Huge granite stones were transported to the site, somehow, cut precisely to construct the structures and water canals to create Machu Picchu, regarded as one of the Seven Wonders of the World. Even more impressive is the Temple of the Sun, elliptical in design with two windows aligning with the summer and winter solstice. These ancient people observed the movement of the sun, stars, and were aware of the constellations. Amazing! Hiking down in the evening, I look up through the forest's canopy to see the Southern Cross above me, bright and imposing, reminding me to celebrate this moment of my life.

At the end of my third day, hiking Machu Picchu, I opt to take an old bus on a narrow, steep, switch-back road. It is one of the most terrifying experiences of my life, as the driver brakes and slides around tight turns. That night, I dreamt I was in a rerun of the *Romancing the Stone* movie. The next day, I opt to take the train back to Cusco, along the raging, whitewater Urubamba River through the Sacred Valley of the Incas. My weary legs thanked me profusely.

On the train, a young woman sits across from me. She resembles my oldest daughter, especially when she smiles. Reaching for my iPhone, I comment that she has a sister in America, and show her a photo of my daughter. She is startled, asking about my ethnic background. When I tell her mostly Hungarian, she begins to cry. "Me, too," she says. She implores me to visit her family in Lima. I do, receiving a warm welcome by her father and older sister. They share their incredible family story of gypsy origins, migrating from Hungary to northern Spain in the early 19th century, living in the Pyrenees Mountains for over a century, then coming to Peru. The old man grabs me by my shoulders and says, "We are family!" We hug and cry. He further tells me that eastern European gypsies migrated to many countries in South America, commenting, *"I guess we are a very long way from home. Once in a while we find each other, as you found my daughter on the train."* We share a meal, photos, stories, and hugs goodbye.

Wonder of the World

Flying north the next day, over the Galapagos Islands, I reflect on my experience in Peru, the towering majesty of the Andes, the incredible trek along the Inca Trail, and the mystical wonder of Machu Picchu. Even so, lingering in my heart is also the memory of distant family lost and found. All incredible gifts in my life.

Along the Beach

Walking alone
along the beach
in the late evening
clears my mind

No thoughts
of politics, religion
sports, family
only fresh ocean air

I sit on the rocks
enjoy nature's symphony
surf, wind, sun, clouds
hint of deep mysteries

I rise and walk
slowly up the beach
gliding with spacetime
in this exquisite moment

As the stars appear
I begin to disappear
in the wonder of it all
beheld in its beauty

I yearn to live
yet another day
another lifetime
to be more possible

Less mortal perhaps
among the gods
just a bit longer
along the beach

REALIZATIONS

Voice

ॐ

Years ago, running along the Willamette River trail in Eugene with a friend who taught creative writing, I mentioned that I was a writer wannabe, but struggled with composition, syntax, and style. Did he have any advice? His response was surprisingly simple: "Find your voice, and everything else will flow together for you." Finding my *voice* seems like a mystical venture. Just what did this mean? I have always enjoyed storytelling, reminiscing about my family history and significant life experiences. My writing, often prolix and unimaginative, was inhibited by a lack of ability. I persisted, believing it was therapeutic for me. As time passed, my *voice* emerged from the mind of an armchair philosopher, reflecting on existential and ethical issues. There were long lapses of time in which my voice was silent, times of pressing commitments and responsibilities. When I would least expect it, however, the urge to write arose, like a haunting whisper in a gentle breeze, often in the dark of night. I have a collection of napkins, notepads, and journals with random reflections, most of which I have hung on to over the years. I have found notes in the bottom of sleeping bags and backpacks, in the pockets of clothes not worn for years, even under the bed or in the wash, completely erased. Some of these reflections are in *Finding Heart* (2012). In all of this literary coming and going, one deeper voice persisted: "Don't stop writing." On a few occasions, my oldest daughter would read my writings and echo the same admonition. So, I continue to listen to my voice and write what it tells me. In the last decade, I have also added the *voice* of a poet and mystic. It is my muse when philosophical reflections become too emotionally draining.

I sit on the lawn at the university, enjoying conversation with some of my students and colleagues. Bright, curious, reflective minds. Life flows so freely in their beings, as they eagerly seek understanding and knowledge. My voice simply asks questions to prompt rigorous analysis, resisting answers, sustaining the sacred space in which learning occurs. Many share their fondest hopes and deepest fears intimately. They reach for meaning, and in the process, discover what truly matters in life.

Mostly, I write for myself alone, finding it insightful to look at my thoughts over time and examine how my views have changed. I *find heart* in such change. I write with the hope that others may enjoy what I have to say, even if they don't necessarily agree with it. I write for future family generations who may discover my words, and *find heart* in them.

Hiking along the top west side of Spencer Butte with my dog, Luke, I pause to drink in the beauty around me. As I stand motionless, my voice begins to speak to me quietly, marveling at the birdsongs in the wind and at the play of sunshine and shadow through the tall firs. I am beheld by a natural world much older than I, and in the grasp of its antiquity and serenity, my fleeting presence reverently pays homage for its gifts.

As I age and life becomes even more vibrant and less lasting, my *voice* is clearer and more frequent. These words are written because my voice is speaking to me, telling me to listen and write, to honor my voice, even if no one but myself is the audience. As I gradually strengthen my prose, my voice whispers: "Sometimes, the best gifts of life are among the last ones we are fortunate enough to receive." Now, I am seriously attempting to become a better writer, even occasionally published, but learning anew.

Wandering along the beach, it beckons me to see and hear, and embrace the wonder around me. I sit on a driftwood log and drink it all in deeply, suspending distracting thoughts, clearing my mind completely, allowing nature to paint on a clean canvas with its own exquisite stroke and touch. Only when I ignore this wonder, and force myself to paint on this canvas, are my words sterile and meaningless.

My *voice* speaks only when it wants to, not when I compel it to speak. It cannot be commanded, only nurtured. Some writers speak of "writer's block," mostly when their voice is being forced to speak. When I have periods in which my voice is silent, I am unconcerned, for I sense it is merely resting and absorbing life experiences, delaying reflection for another day. No rush. When that day surprisingly comes, I am carried away and my head spins. I resist the urge to start writing because it may interrupt my voice. Rather, I patiently listen. As it speaks, I engage in a robust and insightful conversation, rich in detail and critical thinking. Some of what I hear is lost before I can capture it on my computer. My mind also generates a lot of mush which I later ignore. As I grow older, my memory is less able to fully retain all that my voice whispers. No worry. I write as much as I recall, hoping other fragments will resurface in my quiet moments. Later, when I edit what I have written, some lost fragments appear between the lines of what I have written. If not, I am at peace with what I retain.

I sit on a bench in Central Park (New York City) to watch the crowd walk by, to delight in their diverse beauty and energy. A few people join me on the bench and I invite conversation. All are philosophers at heart with their own voices, reaching beyond weather and news, searching for meaning in the flow of life experiences. A quick bond is nurtured, connecting us before we move on. Alone, I succumb to a brief romance with idealism, giving rise to a buoyancy of mystical sensations seemingly connecting with the inexplicable infinite. Or maybe, I enjoy an unwrapped gift of delightful delusions.

My voice will speak until my last breath, and I will continue to write for as long as I can. I hope there is little ego corrupting this venture, only purpose and promise. The purpose is to inspire others to write and tell their life stories. The promise is in *finding heart*, discovering meaning unnoticed in life experiences. A yearning may arise in you to find your *voice*. You may doubt that you have meaningful stories to tell, and when you try to tell them, they may not come easily. Understand that stories and other prose do not appear with a pen and paper in hand, commanding the words to leap from your consciousness. In fact, the pen and paper may only command empty silence. Stories unfold gradually beyond mere memories, reaching deeper, taking us on a philosophical search for meaning, often unapparent in events, places and people. Let the yearning find space and grow deep within you. Leave it alone, to have space. When you least expect it, in sleepless dreams, in tumultuous conflict, in dark hours of pain and suffering, in quiet hours of peaceful meditation, you will enter a space of reflection, even revelation and redemption, in which your stories will emerge as the sun emerges behind the clouds, shining warmth on your face. Then and only then, race to find your pen and paper, and listen to *your voice*: listen, don't think, just listen, and write. Revise and edit later; just listen and write to capture what your *voice* is saying before it fades from your consciousness forever. Once your words are on paper, close your eyes and be grateful for the miracle you are.

Finding My Words

ॐ

Writing is a block of clay

you have vision

you mold, create

step back

walk around

reflect, suffer, groan

let it set awhile

rethink vision less

craft words more

reach beyond.

You give your best maybe

your creation less than imagined

yourself less than imagined

this dance of artist and artwork

finished only by resolve

art annoyingly incomplete

especially after display

fending off critics

knowing better

unsettled still.

Metaphors so magical

generate insight

give and take meaning
words so much more
than clay, paint, sound, movement
linger in themes, style, syntax
meanings found not in language
only somewhere within the writer
storyteller, poet, novelist, essayist
words finally rising to art.

I listen to my inner voice
write and rewrite
well and not well
yet I continue to write
passion finds purpose
imagination finds promise
demons, gods taunt me
finding my words maybe
creating my art
molding my clay.

Live Poets

ॐ

In a New Zealand bar
the "Live Poets" forum
amidst gentle music
laughter, tears, wine, beer
share verse best aloud
meaning deeply revealed
not mere wisdom
nor certain knowledge
but life beautifully exposed.

In contrast, I write
poetry with one finger
on the "Delete" key
painfully sophomoric
content and style
parsimonious wordplay
seemingly philosophic
on a good day
always indolent.

Too often rationalized as
an expedient literary form
caging ideas, emotions
in tightly framed prose

less meaningful experience

searching for insight

more academic babble

quickly defeating its purpose

not poetry after all.

A coffeehouse friend

is amusingly convinced

reading poetry

reveals an intellectual

he is not, confessing

it is confounding, exposing

obscure revelations

seldom found

in daily conversation.

Another friend finds me alone

with a pile of poetry books

in their exquisite embrace

asks for my favorites

I ask for hers

we share together

what speaks to us

takes us deeper

lifts us further.

As I read poetry

from true poets

intimate poignant words

saturate my being

with power, clarity

vividly articulating meaning

arising from life experiences

finding its way to art

finding its way to me.

I hit the "Delete" key often

finally, write these words

share with poet friends live

drink more beer, wine, listen

less to specific editorial review

more to artistic commentary

write and rewrite arduously

crafting my fledgling poetry

a long way from home.

A Simple Life

Oḿ

I enjoy giving my life's litter away as I grow older. Most of my "gifts" are unnecessary things that I have inexplicably kept for no apparent reason, tucked away in the back of my closets, drawers, attics and basements, forgotten, nearly lost. Not for long, however, as I now eagerly bag or box them up and give them away, tending to be the "accelerator" whereas my wife often applies the "brakes," and questions my judgment. She muses that we are a "good balance," otherwise, we may be living out of my backpack.

Generations apart, my parents suffered from the *Great Depression Blues*, hanging on to stuff excessively, like a warm security blanket to comfort and protect them from rainy days and dark nights, from inevitable layoffs and looming poverty. My mother had new towels and linens neatly stored in the back of dressers, nearly new sweaters and coats in the back of closets, countless rolls of toilet paper (that mice destroyed) in the attic, and food supplies (that rats often devoured) in the basement. I could not touch such stuff without a severe scolding. Years later, I would discover such stuff, unused, nearly lost in the catacombs of life.

Even today, many around me accumulate stuff. A lot of stuff! They no longer suffer from the *Great Depression Blues;* rather, they embrace the *Great American Dream*. They walk the shopping malls or surf eBay for entertainment. Wearing new clothes and driving new cars is what our enhanced standard of living is arguably all about. Our society frames our wants, not just needs, as essential. Our values become confused, lost.

I am unlike most people. I seldom define my *self-worth* by my *net worth,* by the things that I own, by my wealth. Over my lifetime, it has weighed on me that I have unused clothes and other stuff in my possession, just sitting out of sight and mind. Surely, there are people in my community who could use it to lighten life's burdens. It seems that, just maybe, the greater good is best served by having less and sharing more.

I wonder why simplicity is so appealing to me. My reflections take me back in time, and I wonder more, not less. When my mother and I moved to California, we stored our furnishings and personal memorabilia in the attic of our rented flat, asking neighbors to protect it until we were able to return for it. A year later, we returned to New York, only to discover that it had all been stolen. Lost was our family history: countless photo albums, collectibles, furniture handmade by my grandfather, everything. I didn't think it mattered much to me, but it did later in life. I longed to see pictures of deceased family members, of my childhood, of friends with whom I grew up, of my past, my roots. Our initial anger for having been wronged was gradually replaced by a deepening sense of sadness and loss, even depression. I learned to live without it, pushing the pain aside.

In California, my mother and I lived very simply in a furnished one-bedroom apartment for two years, until she remarried. Understand that our lifestyle was not so much a matter of philosophy, but a matter of necessity, given our lack of resources. A year later, I served as a Mormon Missionary in Germany, requiring me to travel light and live simply, storing all of our possessions in two suitcases, limited to forty pounds. It taught me that I didn't need much to live and enjoy life. I could live in a small space, and move quickly. Returning to the USA, I would begin a marriage with very little stuff, with only our dreams to keep us warm at night. We ate off paper plates with plastic forks, lived in a cockroach-filled apartment, and worked to return to college in Utah. My wife had only one wool coat and dress to keep her warm in the Utah winter as she carried our first child into the world. In spite of the lack of resources, we were happy together. A very simple life.

As the years rolled by, I confess that I gave in to the accumulation of stuff. Homes were purchased, along with furnishings. Cars were a necessity, not just one, but several. Clothes were stuffed into closets and dressers. Antiques were collected. A library full of books was amassed. More and more stuff. New stuff came into my life, and old stuff was pushed aside, but seldom disposed of. Rather, more space was acquired to store stuff. I wondered if this tendency was "in my blood," that my parents were looking over my shoulder, whispering to me to amass additional things for bad times. We were living the American Dream, and our stuff was often a measure of our success. Conversely, I began sensing a deepening confinement, of being caged by stuff, of even defining my life circumstances by my property. Our standard of living was often measured by comparisons with others around us, an economic race without a finish line, it seemed. Slowly, I came to realize that I was not happy, surrounded by more and more stuff.

I noticed friends around me who lived out their lives with tons of unnecessary stuff, including large homes filled with rooms of furnishings seldom used. They would die, and their families were faced with the burden of disposing of such stuff, most of which was not retained. A sorrowful legacy indeed.

To the surprise of both family and friends, we traveled a different path into retirement. We sold our large family home, sold four cars, and disposed of nearly 90 percent of our stuff. I remember with fondness the day when I saw a man wearing an old suit of mine, as he accompanied his daughter at her marriage. I smiled and even wept a bit. When I see our antiques in the homes of my children, I am filled with the pleasure of knowing what they chose to retain, albeit not much. Even friends mention stuff they took, that we have forgotten. I seldom think about the things that are no longer a part of my life. Even though my library is gone now, the authors of many of those books remain my "friends" and talk to me still. More importantly, I live a simple life at the beach, where we have become our dream. We endeavor to not bring anything into our space without taking something out, giving it away.

The simple life is the best life for me. Stress, work, and expense are minimal. Freedom and resources expand. It seems moral to live a simple life, to recognize when enough is enough, to travel light, to focus on what truly matters.

Note: Living in a 1,200-foot beach cottage with two bedrooms and two baths is perfect for us at this time of our lives: simple, quiet, and low maintenance.

On Generosity

(reflections for my grandchildren)

You may say a little
about your grandfather
or much less in time
all okay, no worries

You know one
thing for sure
he was generous
supporting you

Your dreams
mattered to him
you truly became
your dreams

Don't ever
forget his example
use it as a torch
held high to help

You will be older
even a grandparent

share what you have

be generous

Give not only

resources, but

time, patience

love above all

Know finally

you will be

living a life

that matters

Never Grow Up

༊

A part of me will never grow up, never age, never change. This part of me seldom takes life too seriously, inviting playful engagement and whimsical lightheartedness. It is inpatient, relentless, sentient, spontaneous, even adolescent. I muse life may unfold as a cartoon strip in which we play out the comedy of our lives. Being conservatively mature compromises being, causing us to miss much of value, promise, and hope. It daydreams when confronted with the mundane. It finds wit when confronted with nonsense.

This part of me invites others to join me in play. Absorbing their excitement and energy, my weary body renews itself and reaches deep to stretch my more willing spirit. It is my favorite pastime, the pure delight of joyful engagement. I hope that all of my days will allow good humor and cheer. Only when I ignore this part of me, am I truly old, and my life nearly over.

Even when alone in the wilderness, I find this part of my being yearning for release. Joining in the flow of nature, jumping from cliffs into rivers, climbing trees high in the wind, dancing with sunshine in wildflower meadows, singing songs with birds, sharing my poetry with small creatures, allowing the rain to cleanse me as it washes the earth—originates in this part of me. It is woven into the fabric of my being, a fabric connecting me with life on earth. Have you ever noticed that animals play? Birds chase each other? Flowers greet the morning sun and afternoon rain? Clouds test imagination? Grass tickles our feet? Breezes sneak kisses? Can you see: This part of me is a part of all that is?

Have you sensed this part of yourself? It is there somewhere. Have you invited it to come out to play?

Gratitude fills me when I realize that I will never grow up. I would never allow it, even if I could. I am unashamed, unembarrassed by my playfulness. It may be rooted in my childhood, a time when I did not have much playtime, being an only child in an adult environment. Understand that there is no tolerance for sarcasm, embarrassment or ridicule. And if it occurs in the flow of playfulness, there is no excuse, only regret.

Grandchildren at Beach

This part of me is most lasting. I will shed the remainder of my being first. I will smile when the deep mystery calls me home.

So, to my family, remember that I played with you in so many countless ways, to invite smiles and laughter, before another day passed by unnoticed, forever.

Facing the Fear

ୡ

Friends wonder about my sanity in moving from a high, secure elevation south of Eugene, Oregon to a northern coastal location near the beach. In recent years, there have been frequent reports of the "Big One," describing a major earthquake followed by a devastating tsunami along the Pacific Rim. Scientific research clearly predicts that it is not only overdue but likely to cause widespread damage and loss of life. Most of the coastal communities will be destroyed.

In the face of such reports, I moved to Cannon Beach. Decades ago, my wife and I mused that it would be our dream to retire here, walking the beaches and enjoying the small community. We have not been disappointed. Unlike Eugene where we lived in the country and had few neighbors, and Portland where we lived in a vibrant urban setting with limited neighbor contact, our small beach community has been more fulfilling.

We face the possibility of not surviving a catastrophic event. Even so, we choose to set it aside in daily living, believing that we will do the best to survive, and be as fully prepared as possible. Others in the community may indeed be in denial, claiming that reports are overstated and the "event" is unlikely in our lifetime. The ground will shake, homes and roads will be damaged, and waves will overwhelm us. The prospect of loss is unimaginable yet manageable perhaps. We smile and avoid serious debate. We accept whatever comes and goes.

Why? Because this is our life, the life we choose. We live with the risk because the beauty of this place is worth it, the wonder of each walk along the beach, each sunset, each peaceful summer day, and each stormy winter day. Hand in hand, we laugh and embrace life here in its fullness, even our love for each other.

No matter what! Life will go on, and hopefully, we will enjoy our life for some time. But if it ends tomorrow, we are at peace. When one considers the prospect of natural death late in life, it seems easier to cope, given the tradeoffs. To live in a place of beauty and peace, removed from urban clutter, congestion and crime, I am willing to accept my fate, whatever and whenever.

To my friends who are dismayed at what they consider my willful stupidity, I smile and face fear. We have our emergency backpacks and have practiced our evacuation routes. Dark reality is overshadowed by my happiness in this place, with my beautiful woman at my side, and with my visiting family (though I hope they will be spared the "event"). Sustained by my shared memories and dreams, I say to my friends: "It is ok and we are ok. It is what it is. And we will do our best to do what we need to do. No worries."

Just You and Me

ॐ

Life flows forward on the steady stream of time. And we drift along with it. No matter what, it keeps flowing and we keep drifting. Time and change are the only constants.

Over fifty years ago, we came together on an impulse, filled with dreams and resolve. We have journeyed a long way together, *just you and me.*

Our children came into the world and we endeavored to shape their values and beliefs, to raise them well. At times, we succeeded, and at times, we failed. Our children gave us joy and heartache. At times, we blamed them, and at times, we blamed ourselves, and with age, we expunged blame. We were haunted by retrospective guilt about things we could have done better. We wish we could have been better parents. We grew old together trying our very best to love well.

In the end, due to or in spite of our efforts, our children chose their own paths, made their own choices, and experienced their own journeys. At times, we were guides or muses, and at times, we were obstacles. Mostly, we were mere spectators. Our hearts were always in play, cheering them on, lifting them up, hoping for the very best.

They brought children into the world and strived to raise them well, at times succeeding or failing. We sought to support our family. Sometimes, we did, and sometimes, we failed. Sometimes, they did well; sometimes, they failed. They experienced joy and pain. When our hearts ached in the quiet hours of our life together, we knew, it was *just you and me.*

Due to or in spite of our efforts, our grandchildren chose their own paths, too, made their own decisions, and are experiencing their journeys. History often repeats itself. We smile and we cry. We take deep breaths, hug, and move on.

The cycles and seasons of life persist. We grow old. We look back and wonder: why? What could we have done differently? Better? We will never know. We don't need to know. Our gods and demons mess with us. Their voices haunt us, but we push them aside and move on, *just you and me.*

We know only that we tried to raise them well. When things went right or wrong, it was *not* our fault. They made choices; we did not.

We are now minor players on the field of family life. Whatever happens, happens. We wish our family well. They try to tell us they are ok, but our doubts persist. We celebrate their accomplishments, but we witness their pain and disappointments. It is *not* our fault. We know they will survive. And they know we love them.

We begin to recognize that life is what it is. It may be to our credit if they experience some measure of happiness. We cannot take credit and it's *not* our fault if they experience heartache. We cannot be alive and ignore their lives. So, we will love them, patiently and compassionately, provide resources to the fullest extent we can, and hope for the very, very best.

Time and change are not the only constants, so is *love*. It has endured, even when we are suffering from exhaustion. Time and change, though constant, will not endure. Love will, even if unnoticed, even when we have to forgive ourselves for acts of love. In the end, what endures is *just you and me.*

There are a few things that I wish to personally say to my children and grandchildren as you read my words. I appreciate your expressions of love, saying that I was a good man. I know that there were times when that was not the case. In the sunset of my life, I choose to define myself by my best moments and memories. Those best moments are far more abundant in my life. Those are the ones that deeply reveal my character and my love for you. I hope you define me by those best moments. And forgive my worst.

A few other clarifications of my personal philosophy:

I respect and defend your right to have free speech. However, I may or may not respect your opinion. I have always sought to challenge you to fully understand how opinions are formed, and to critically think about them. At times, you may have been annoyed by my persistent questioning or for pushing books at you. Forgive me for these acts of love.

I respect and defend your right to choose the person you become and the life you create. However, I may or may not respect your thinking underlying those choices, and challenge you to critically think about them. No, I am not trying to tell you what to do, imposing my expectations upon you. I merely want you to deeply reflect upon your philosophy of life. Forgive me for this act of love.

I understand that our time together will diminish as we grow older, as you become more independent and immersed in your life. I will miss our time together but accommodating your space of growth is important to me. Forgive me for this separation, for this act of love.

There is much more philosophy that flows in my being, waiting for another day, another act of love.

Her Laughter

ॐ

My life companion loves to laugh. Sometimes, spontaneously out loud. Good humor. Sometimes, quietly in her smile and eyes. Always an invitation to join her, to passionately embrace the comedy of life.

On our first date, she entertained me at the movies. Listening to her easy laughter was a delight in itself. She immersed herself in the experience completely, laughing openly, spontaneously, unapologetically. Her laughter relaxed me, opened me, softened me.

Observing her in social settings, she engages others easily, seasoning conversations with an infectious smile and gentle laughter. Along for the ride, I hang on tightly, enjoying it fully. She makes friends quickly, intimately, lastingly.

As children entered our life, I watched her lift them into her arms and smile. In her smile, her sense of goodness would transmigrate into their being. Their laughter would come as easily as hers, as they played and grew into adulthood.

In times of pain, her unspoken faith was transparent in her smile and her healing power in her laughter. Others might despair, but not her, not even for a moment. Her spirit would transcend any pain, focusing on the positive, lifting others with her. No need for advice, only empathy. She would give birth to miracles, over and over again.

Whenever others close to her became discouraged, she would light up their darkness, renewing them with her laughter, hugging them tightly, and looking directly into their eyes, affirming what mattered most in life. Her laughter was never offensive; only a gentle reminder for life balance. For me, engaging in good-spirited laughter with her became more uplifting than meditation, therapy or religious experiences. In my quiet hours, she is my muse.

Most of us enjoy the power of positive thinking and energy, along with exchanges filled with smiles and laughter. Her engaging laughter was much different than most other people, more amazing. I still witness it after five decades and smile. It warms hearts, dissipating the chilling draft of mortality. Only when I am absent from her good cheer and her buoyant spirit, do I fully realize the space she alone fills. She lifts me from the ground of serious philosophical contemplation into the fresh air of happy-heartedness.

Found

ॐ

Whenever I seek heart
I find it only fleetingly.
Whenever I embrace life fully
heart is abundantly found.

My father's God spoke to me
blessing me in ways least expected.

The haunting stories of my grandfather
preserving family history and legacy.

My children taught me to be
a better husband and father.

I played with my grandchildren at the beach
watching them grow beautifully.

Whenever I seek to fashion
meaningful life experiences
only modest success is achieved.

Whenever I invite the prospect
of wider-ranging life experiences
so much more is found.

An old couple reached out to help
in the middle of nowhere, in the middle of night.

Distant family was found in Peru
from a young woman on a train.

Young Nepali children took me home
allowing me to embrace their family.

Canyon walls, raging rivers, high mountains
took me home to a place I hadn't been before.

I confess immense joy
arising spontaneously, surprisingly
sustaining a purposeful life
when heart is found.

Poems for Her

ॐ

Talk to me

In an instant
I am gone

You remain behind
with a life filled
with shared joys
and sufferings
now you will create
a new life alone

No need for long grieving
I feel your hand in mine
the sparkle in your blue eyes
your kind smile and touch
though my presence will fade
my love will sustain you

Talk to me
in the quiet of night
light a candle
play some gentle music
and share your heart
with me

I will listen

we will be again

I am here still

Just You and Me

A few last words

You are my final hope
not some religious belief
nor some philosophical idea
just you alone

I feel your hand in mine
look into your blue eyes
enjoy your sweet smile
your gentle touch
together we have
come a long way
a very long way

Hope will slip away
with my last breath unnoticed
my memory of our life together
will linger lastly
it will sustain, comfort me
in the darkness
and if by some miracle
light lifts me from extinction
you will be in the light again

For the Rest of Your Life

You can read my words
when I'm gone
you can know my heart
and let me hold you again
Not forever
but in this quiet moment
you will feel my love
for the rest of your life

I will find you

when least expected
early awakenings
beautiful encounters
deepest yearnings
darkest pain
quiet of night

I will
find you

an old song
on the radio
an old photo
in a forgotten place

an old memory

in a new time

I will

find you

Even when

walking on the beach

sitting on a park bench

celebrating with loved ones

moments alone at home

under a starry night sky

I will

find you

You and me

will be again

Growing Old

ॐ

Read whatever books you like
in the middle of the night,
write as much as you like
about whatever you damn well like.

Listen to whatever music you like
for as long and loud as you like,
watch Casablanca and African Queen
with as many snacks as you like.

Do absolutely nothing whenever
for as long as you like,
nap naked as often as you like
for as long as you damn well like.

Wear old worn clothes you like
on every last day of your life if you like,
hang out with friends at coffee shops
argue endlessly about whatever you like.

Eat and drink whenever whatever you like
without ever heeding your conscience,
stay in the hot shower as long as you like
whenever you like and then some.

Explore the world as much as you like
wherever and as often as you like,
watch sunrises, sunsets, and starry skies
whenever as long and as often as you like.

Argue with the gods whenever you like
about whatever you damn well like,
hug loved ones as much as you like
whenever you like as long as you like.

Grow old with grace and gratitude
with an attitude to damn death,
embrace your last years joyfully
hopefully for as long as you like.

All in All

ॐ

It has been a good life, all in all.

Growing up in a poor, ethnic neighborhood in upstate New York, I was surrounded by a loving family who influenced my growth with wisdom and patience.

They taught me to work hard, to think clearly, to feel deeply, to tell the truth, and to never fear any idea or person. My father whispers still: it is what it is; you got to do what you got to do; make the best of it; don't bellyache; enjoy what you have.

Being an only child, I knew loneliness intimately. My family taught me to embrace my time alone to think about what matters most and to fill it with a good heart.

At seventeen, I alone coped with my father's death, took care of my suffering mother, and found a new life in California. People along the way gave me abundant gifts of kindness.

The best fortune of my life was to meet a beautiful woman who loved me for my entire life, in spite of my faults and shortcomings. No matter what happened, she stood strong.

She taught me to love completely, and to embrace her love completely, creating a union that withstood the challenges and complications of life.

To my great joy, I fathered three wonderful children and loved seven wonderful grandchildren. They taught me so much, and loved me so incredibly well.

My wife shared her deepest dreams, and I endeavored to make them all come true. Together, we raised a wonderful family, built our country home, followed our hearts to many places, and spent our sunset years at the beach.

I met remarkable people along the way. They shared their ideas, affection, kindness, and trust. Their friendships enriched my life so immensely.

I sit on a porch above the city of Nelson, New Zealand, my wife writing note cards close by. The air is warm, the sky is blue, the sun is drifting toward the western horizon, the gentle breeze is full of floral fragrances, the birds are singing, and the beauty of nature is holding me in its close embrace. The night sky will soon teach me again.

It has been a good life, all in all.

OLD FRIENDS

Old Friends

ঙ

I

When I was a boy, I hated the sight of a book. Going to the dentist or drinking cod liver oil (medicine) were more pleasant thoughts. I was "reading challenged" because English was my second language, and though I mostly spoke and understood it, I could not read or write it well. However, books were all around our home, thanks to my father and grandfather. They were self-educated men, and both consumed books vigorously. When we sat around relaxing or eating meals, books were gladly received guests. Our conversations quickly moved from sports or work to philosophical or political ones. Of course, my family patiently included me in such discussions, asking questions, listening to my ideas, and inviting me to read from their books. Such involvement was torturous. Books would regularly appear next to my bed or on my desk. It was not enough to read them (or pretend to); they wanted a report on what I read.

During those early years, any book that I read became mine to place in the small bookcase in my bedroom. I accumulated about thirty books before high school work (age fourteen) took precedence. Of particular interest were books focusing on the basics of western philosophy. Having these books, I noticed that they spoke to me at times, reminding me of what I read, especially if some relevant insight could be garnered. After high school in New York, I found myself moving to California, working and going to college. My apartment furnishings were incomplete without a bookcase. Once obtained, it started filling up with books, mostly from used bookstores or college classes. Compared to other college students, my reading ability and vocabulary were clearly marginal, but I nevertheless acquired a love of books and a passion to read them, albeit slowly with a dictionary in hand.

II

In my early twenties, I lived as a Mormon missionary in Germany for several years and was required to limit my wardrobe to two suitcases. Unlike my companions, I limited it to a single suitcase, and loaded books into the second one. They were my true companions. Thanks to my grandfather, I had a deep interest in western philosophy, and living in Europe, I started reading some of the most recognized authors. First, however, was **Albert** Schweitzer, *Geschichte des Leben Jesu Forschung* (The Quest for the Historical Jesus). It was recommended by a friend, a Lutheran theologian, who after I read the book and discussed its contents with him, bound the volume in leather as a gift to me (it is still in my possession). **Albert** informed me that there was serious doubt, given the lack of historical evidence, that Jesus Christ even existed. It seemed that I could read German better than English as its grammar made more logical sense to me. The process of reading philosophy books in German was similar to the process I used to learn to read English as a boy with a dictionary in hand. In 1963, I enrolled in a Survey of Philosophy class at the University of Cologne, covering major European philosophers. It was a trip down memory lane, as many of them were mentioned in **Will** Durant, *Story of Philosophy*, a book that I had read with my grandfather when I was eleven to twelve-years-old. The course did not use a survey textbook, but rather assigned sections of major works: **Rene** Descartes, *Discourse on Method and* Meditations; **Baruch** Spinoza, *Ethics*; G.W. Leibniz, *Discourse on Metaphysics*; **John** Locke, *An Essay Concerning Human Understanding*; **Immanuel** Kant, *Critique of Pure Reason*; **Friedrich** Nietzsche, *Thus Spoke Zarathustra*; **Jean-Paul** Sartre, *Being and Nothingness* and *Existentialism and Human Emotions*; **Martin** Heidegger, *Existence and Being* and *Being and Time*; and several others which escape my recollection. Somehow, **Aristotle**, *Nicomachean Ethics* found its way into our study. I purchased copies of these texts and stored them in my second suitcase under my bed, to elude detection from my missionary companions who mostly viewed philosophy as a threat to religion. Over the course of the next two years in Germany, I added twenty philosophy books to my collection, filling every inch of my second suitcase. Even better, I formed friendships with Germans who were well versed in these texts, allowing for many insightful conversations. Philosophy was clearly in my bloodstream, flowing through my brain in my quiet moments, even in my sleep. Religion was flowing out, especially after reading **Friedrich**, who seriously challenged religious dogma.

The survey course opened the door to a more expansive, serious study of philosophy. I was fascinated by the vast range of issues that philosophy addressed, always with candor and clarity. It attacked ideas vigorously, attempting to construct sound arguments based on verifiable facts, good logic (validity), and sound judgment. While many of the perspectives (especially metaphysics) of western philosophers were influenced by historical context and are largely outdated today, I discovered many that were indeed relevant and worthy of further study. Many questioned the religious and political aspects of society around them, often expressing skepticism and concern. Nietzsche and Sartre were particularly impressive; yet, I admittedly had reservations with much that I read. I was starting to develop my own philosopher's voice.

The first names of my "old friends" are in **bold**; later in life, I came to whimsically call them by their first (formal) names as they whispered to me. Most authors are not bolded; only those whose thoughts I recalled often.

III

I returned to the USA, thinking that it would take less than two years to obtain my BS degree, and then I could return to Europe and pursue a PhD in Philosophy or Mathematics, maybe becoming a professor some day. While that didn't happen, my passion for philosophy remained strong. I began to read several survey texts (20+), followed by a more detailed study of individual philosophers and related issues; the most significant survey texts of interest to me were: Robert Solomon, *From Rationalism to Existentialism*; Arthur Minton and Thomas Shipka, *Philosophy: Paradox and Discovery;* Frank Magill (Editor), *Masterpieces of World Philosophy*; Chris Rohmann, *A World of Ideas*; Philip Stokes, *Philosophy: 100 Essential Thinkers*; Ted Honderich (Editor), *The*

Oxford Guide to Philosophy; James Russell (Editor), *Philosophical Classics: The Thinking Person's Guide to Great Philosophical Books*; Tom Butler-Bowdon, *50 Philosophy Classics*; and Christopher Phillip, *Socrates Café: A Fresh Taste of Philosophy*. I also collected a wider range of additional works (100+) by the major European and American philosophers. During this period, I came to value philosophical analysis as a tool for critical thinking; my skepticism was deepening.

Along the way, I read **Daniel** Dennett, *Consciousness Explained*, reread **Rene** Descartes, *Meditations on First Philosophy,* and **Georg** Hegel, *Phenomenology of Spirit*, and developed a lifelong interest in the nature of *consciousness* (and the emergence of human cognition and intelligence). Later in life, probably the most influential philosopher was again **Daniel** Dennett, *Sweet Dreams*, and to a lesser degree **Thomas** Nagel, *Mind and Cosmos*. (I acquired over thirty volumes focusing on consciousness over the years.) I also took an intellectual sojourn into eastern philosophy, focusing on consciousness (and idealism). I was drawn to the study of consciousness, the philosopher's theoretical equivalence to the physicist's engagement of quantum gravity, both confounding unknowns. Throughout my later life, the study of consciousness has caused me to rethink the neo-Darwinist materialistic view of the universe, albeit infrequently, wondering if it is too limited in scope. Yet, in the face of unknown, my intellectual default option was philosophical skepticism. Within my religious community, I was viewed as a heretic (or worse), so my conversations were mostly limited to my new *friends* and University colleagues.

I also better framed my personal philosophy of life: Corliss Lamont, *The Philosophy of Humanism*; and **Paul** Kurtz, *The Humanist Manifesto*. Humanism appealed to my intellectual sensibilities. It placed a supreme value on the good life, on doing the right thing. It set religion aside as a foundation for ethics. It challenged prevailing metaphysical assertions, not only replete in religion but common in society. Of most importance, it viewed the person as a responsible, independent, moral being. While humanism never evolved into a dominant force, it remained a strong influence in my life, as a more reasonable perspective than those advocated by religions.

All of these books were added to my growing personal library, and in 1976, I built a home with ample bookshelves to place them in front of me, as I reflected on my deepest thoughts and engaged in my most meaningful conversations.

IV

I failed in compartmentalizing my life into a private passion for philosophy and a public commitment for religion. In the face of growing cognitive dissonance and emotional stress, I began to read authors who focused on the philosophy of religion; my favorites were: Blaise Pascal, *Pensees*; Ian Barbour, *Issues in Science and Religion*; Jerry Gill, *Philosophy and Religion*; **Steven** Cahn, *Philosophy of Religion*; **Dietrich** Bonhoeffer, *Creation and Fall, Temptation*; **Huston** Smith, *The World Religions*; Gardner Murphy, *Asian Psychology and Religion*; **Walter** Kaufmann, *The Faith of a Heretic* and *The Passover Plot*; **William** James, *The Varieties of Religious Experience*; **Sigmund** Freud, *The Future of an*

Illusion; **Thomas** O'Dea, *Alienation, Atheism and the Religious Crisis;* Ronald Santoni, *Religious Language and the Problem of Religious Knowledge;* **Ram** Dass, *The Only Dance That Is;* James Pike, *If This Be Heresy;* John Robinson, *Honest to God;* **James** Carse, *Breakfast At The Victory: The Mysticism of Ordinary Experience;* Sogyal Rinpoche, *The Tibetan Book of Living and Dying;* Kelly Clark, *Philosophers Who Believe;* Revel Jean-Francois, *The Monk and the Philosopher;* and **Somerset** Maugham, *The Summing Up.* Over 200 volumes focusing on the philosophy or history of religion were added to my library over twenty years, and a few of my favorites were: **Joseph** Pearce, *The Crack in the Cosmic Egg;* **Dalai Lama**, *The Universe in a Single Atom* and *Toward a Kinship of Faiths;* Mohammad Klan, *The Quran;* **Paul** Tillich, *My Search for Absolutes* and *Dynamics of Faith;* **Sterling** McMurrin, *Matters of Conscience* and *Religion, Reason, and Truth: Historical Essays in the Philosophy of Religion;* Harold Schulweis, *For Those Who Can't Believe;* Henri de Botton, *The Religion of Teilhard de Chardin;* Sharon Salzberg, *Faith: Trusting Your Own Deepest Experiences;* Donald Wells, *God, Man, and the Thinker: Philosophies of Religion;* Ken Wilbur, *The Marriage of Sense and Soul: Integrating Science and Religion;* **John** O'Donohue, *Anam Cara* and *To Bless The Space Between Us;* Vincent Buglios *Divinity of Doubt;* Michael Krasny, *Spiritual Envy: An Agnostic's Quest;* Armand Nicholi, *The Question of God: C.S. Lewis and Sigmund Freud Debate;* **Gary** Synder, *The Practice of the Wild;* Richard Tarnas, *Cosmos and Psyche: Intimations of a New World View:* and Christian Wiman, *My Bright Abyss: Mediation of a Modern Believer.* During this time, my spouse was lovingly patient and impatient, patient in allowing me to retreat into my study of philosophy, and impatient in desiring a stronger leap of religious faith. The latter would only disingenuously appear to support family aims.

It seemed that the more I read about the philosophy of religion, the more I questioned metaphysical presumptions, especially those of traditional religions based in ancient views, but also those of early western philosophers who focused on metaphysics. Even so, more modern perspectives did indeed give reason for pause and ponder, whether my skepticism ran too deep and whether a willing suspension of disbelief was reasonable to permit a modest leap of religious faith, albeit prudent and sensible. I seriously doubted the existence of God (and all of the other common metaphysical assertions so associated). Agnosticism appealed to me intellectually, for it seemed that most religious ideas were beyond our epistemological reach, and we could not determine whether there was or was not a God. Atheism, however, appealed to me emotionally, for it seemed that the heavy weight of human suffering and injustice crushed the possibility of a loving supreme entity or life force; in my most intimate moments, I was haunted by my father's death (see His Smile, *Finding Heart* (2012)). In the end, it was a matter of estimated probabilities. It seemed more probable that God did not exist, but also highly probable that reality is more complex, peculiar, and perplexing than we can imagine, even with our best science, justifying my deep skepticism. Slim probabilities generated "hopeful doubt," that there might be some cosmic connection to our being (or consciousness), evident in some alternative way, albeit fleeting and oblique. I entertained Pascal's Wager as an argument for believing, but needed more reason for choosing belief over disbelief. My agnostic's voice told me that I will never know nor do I need to. I could live a good life without God or religion.

V

In 1972, I studied in the Graduate Program in Philosophy at the University of Minnesota, focusing primarily on analytic philosophy to sharpen my skills as a critical thinker, and reading: Robert Ammerman, *Classics of Analytic Philosophy*; **Bertrand** Russell, *The Problems of Philosophy* and *On Denoting (essay)*; **Ludwig** Wittgenstein, *The Blue and Brown Books* and *The Philosophical Investigations*; K.T. Fann, *Wittgenstein's Conception of Philosophy*; **Alfred** Ayer, *Language, Truth and Logic* and *The Problems of Knowledge*; and **Alfred** North Whitehead, *Adventure of Ideas*. Based on this interest, much later was a sojourn into deconstructionism: **Jacques** Derrida, *On Grammatology*; and Christopher Norris, *Deconstruction Theory and Practice*.

Because of the torturous rigor of analytical philosophy, I began to view philosophy through a different set of lenses. Language was the primary issue; it was a human invention to construct meaning with symbols, a very imprecise and flawed invention indeed. Examining language (and grammar) used to express ideas and develop arguments was a tedious, laborious endeavor. It was driven by the moral imperative to make sense out of the nature of reality and being. I discovered that many philosophical issues were merely language problems, that confusion resided in the imprecise use of language, not in the conceptual merit of an idea. I found myself surrounded by meaningless statements, and some of my foundational arguments were unsound. It was time to seek higher ground. My *friends* were smiling. Even so, **Karl** Popper, *The Logic of Scientific Discovery,* provided me with some intellectual balance in the face of linguistic and logical analytics.

Notwithstanding my religious sojourns, I tended to respect my deeper original philosophical biases: **Bertrand** Russell, *Why I am Not a Christian*; **Richard** Dawkins, *The God Delusion* and *The Greatest Show on Earth: The Evidence for Evolution*; **Christopher** Hitchen, *God is not Great: How Religion Poisons Everything* and *The Portable Atheist: Essential Readings for the Nonbeliever*; Victor Stenger, *God: The Failed Hypothesis*; Louise Antony, *Philosophers Without Gods: Meditations on Atheism and the Secular Life*; Dan Barker, *Godless: How an Evangelical Preacher Became One of America's Leading Atheists*, Stephen Batchelor, *Confessions of a Buddhist Atheist*; Robin LePoldevin, *Arguing for Atheism*; George Smith, *Atheism: The Case Against God;* **Edward** Wilson, *Consilience: The Unity of Knowledge* and *The Meaning of Human Existence*; and **Sam** Harris *End of Faith*.

As a young boy, religious tradition mattered whereas religious belief, though emphasized in my catechism, was less essential in living a good life. My father's premature death provoked rage toward God for this unjust flaw in the divine scheme, inviting atheism to embrace the primal core of my being. As time passed and reflection deepened, the secular life appealed to me as more authentic and honest, even if atheism was less salient. I read the foregoing authors to confirm what I already "knew" and to distance myself from serious religious considerations. While the arguments of these authors were premised with substantial empirical evidence and supported by impeccable logic,

I was haunted by a higher ignorance of the unknown. Listening to my father's gentle voice, I converted it (as he did) into a profound reverence, wonder and awe for the "something" (rather than "nothing") in which we are immersed, recognizing that our imagination is far less robust (along with our epistemological capacities) than the deep mysteries dancing playfully around us.

VI

To create some intellectual balance, I ventured into the philosophy of science, reading **Thomas** Kuhn, *The Structure of Scientific Revolutions*; **Carl** Sagan, *The Varieties of Scientific Experience*; Timothy Ferris, *Coming of Age in the Milky Way*; and John Barrow, *The Anthropic Cosmological Principle*. Later, I would read **Alexander** Rosenberg, *The Philosophy of Social Science,* and **John** Searle, *The Construction of Social Reality*, wonderful gifts, which allowed me to better focus my academic interests and theory building. In recent years, I expanded my interest to theoretical physics and biology (since it bumps into metaphysics): Brian Green, *The Fabric of the Cosmos*; **Stephen** Hawking, *A Brief History of Time*; Lawrence Krauss, *A Universe from Nothing*; David Deutsch, *The Beginning of Infinity: Explanations That Transform the World*; **Daniel** Dennett, *Darwin's Dangerous Ideas*; Max Tegmark, *Our Mathematical Universe*; **Alan** Lightman, *The Accidental Universe*; and **Carlo** Rovelli, *Reality Is Not What It Seems*. I imagine that this intellectual candle was originally lit by **Carl** Sagan.

It seems that there is a cognitive region in which theoretical physics and philosophical metaphysics overlap. Just as scientific discoveries stir the physicist's imagination, it continues to leave ample open space for metaphysics to flourish, and for ontological and cosmological reflections. However, contemporary philosophers are cautious not to venture too far, as they are reminded of the history of philosophy, filled with discredited metaphysics based on our knowledge today. Even so, it is a delightful exercise to engage in metaphysical speculation, even if only to fantasize about the surprises awaiting us (or not) in the vast unknown.

VII

As religion evaporated from my being, I recognized the need to independently construct an ethical framework upon which to ground my philosophy of life, so I studied a diverse sampling of works: **Confucius**, *Analects*; Jean-Jacques Rousseau, *The Social Contract*; **John** Rawls, *A Theory of Justice*; John Mothershead, *Ethics*; Paul Ramsey, *Nine Modern Moralists*; Iris Murdoch, *The Sovereignty of Good*; **Friedrich** Nietzsche, *Beyond Good and Evil*; Amartya Sen, *The Idea of Justice*; **John** Stuart Mill, *On Liberty*; **Peter** Singer, *The Life You Can Save* and *Practical Ethics*; Andre Comte-Sponville, *A Small Treatise on the Great Virtues*; Mark Matousek, *Ethical Wisdom: What Makes Us Good*; Jacob Needleman, *Why Can't We Be Good*; Michael Sandel, *Justice: What's the Right Thing to Do?*; Slavoj Zizek, *Living in the End of Times*; **Sam** Harris, *The Moral Landscape*; and **Kathleen** Dean Moore, *Moral Ground*. In the end, from categorical moral imperatives to utilitarian concerns to moral pragmatism, I find a voice calling me back to my roots, listening to my father extol the ethical ideas of **Aristotle**, and encouraging me to live a virtuous life, honoring truth, justice, beauty, goodness, and love. More recently, I was refreshed by **Sarah** Bakewell, *At the Existential Café: Freedom, Being, and Apricot Cocktails*. In my deepest ethical reflections, I am drawn back to existentialism because it honors my self-determination and freedom, and I alone can decide what is truly right in my life. In considering societal justice, I was mostly impressed that freedom mattered in the best societies, but not without creating expanding opportunities and enhancing fair chances for all. Unless a person's actions harm others directly, they must be protected and permitted, thus enhancing personal freedom.

VIII

Understand that these books did not simply collect dust on my bookshelves. I would find myself thinking about a particular topic or issue, only to recall a relevant discussion in one of my books. These philosophers were talking directly to me, and our *friendship* was constantly rekindled. It became so intellectually fulfilling that I didn't want to wait for them to remind me of our past visits; rather, I began reading books consisting of collections of philosophical classics or surveys of contemporary issues in philosophy: **Bertrand** Russell, *A History of Western Philosophy*; **Walter** Kaufmann, *Existentialism: From Dostoevsky to Sartre*; Frederick Copleston, *A History of Philosophy: The British Philosophers from Berkeley to Hume*; Jostein Gaarder, *Sophie's World*; Gary Kessler, *Voices of Wisdom: A Multicultural Philosophy Reader*; James Russell, *Philosophical Classics: The Thinking Person's Guide to Great Philosophical Books*; George Lakoff and Mark Johnson, *Philosophy in the*

Flesh; Steven Landsburg, *The Big Questions*; Bryan Magee, *Confessions of a Philosopher: A Journey through Western Philosophy*; Will Buckingham, *The Philosophy Book: Big Ideas Explained*; Simon Blackburn, *Think: A Compelling Introduction to Philosophy*; Martyn Oliver, *History of Philosophy*; Stanley Rosen, *Philosophy 101: Selections from the Works of the Western World's Greatest Thinkers*; and Jeremy Stangroom, *The Great Philosophers: From Socrates to Foucault.*

Entertaining the exaggerated notion that a person's character is defined by the books they read, I treasure my library. But it is not my books so much as their authors who speak to me, and they have become my *old friends* as we exchange our innermost thoughts. It would be a tragedy indeed if I did not share their wisdom with others. Often friends learn of my passion for philosophy, ask questions, and a book or two are loaned out. I have loaned out over 100 books, and most of them were never returned. No worries; and no need for library record keeping. A few were replaced. In most cases, reading the books led to conversations about hard questions, weak answers, more questions, unsound arguments, and more reading. I have many fond memories of such conversations with university associates and students as well as intellectually adventurous friends and family. Such conversations have lasted hours, days, and in a few cases, a lifetime. But philosophy is much more than an intellectual play toy, it is *a higher art* in which we create our best ideas and arguments. It transforms strong egos into humble seekers.

Critical, reflective thinking along with the development of sound arguments (i.e. facts, logic, and judgment) is the bedrock of philosophy. Some of my best friends who have helped me to develop my analytical tools are: David Ley, *Tools of Critical Thinking (Metathoughts for Psychology)*; Scott Plous, *The Psychology of Judgment and Decision Making*; Julian Bagginit and Peter Fosi, *The Philosopher's Toolkit*; Robert Sternberg, *Why Smart People Can Be So Stupid*; Thomas Gilovich, *How We Know What Isn't So*; **Dan** Ariely, *Irrational Predictability*; Carol Tavris and Elliot Aronson, *Mistakes Were Made: How We Justify Foolish Beliefs, Bad Decisions, and Hurtful Acts*; **Daniel** Kahneman, *Thinking, Fast and Slow*; Stephen Law, *Believing Bullshit: How Not to Get Sucked into an Intellectual Black Hole*; Gary Harrison, *Think: Why You Should Question Everything*; **Jonah** Lehrer, *How We Decide*; Brooks Jackson and Kathleen Hall Jamieson, *un-Spun: Finding facts in a world of disinformation*; Robert Gula, *Nonsense: How We Abuse Logic in our Everyday Language*; Ali Almossawi, *Bad Arguments*; and Julian Baggini, *The Pig That Wants to Be Eaten: 100 Experiments for the Armchair Philosopher*. Most of these books were in a bibliography I provided to my UO students to sharpen their critical thinking skills at the beginning of the term. Certainly, philosophy is ultimately about ideas, but to develop ideas well requires these methods and skills. Over the course of the last three decades, my most frequent conversations were with these philosophers and psychologists to thoroughly critique my own thoughts and biases.

Philosophers are often viewed as residing in more shadow than light, as stuck in pessimism rather than optimism. People less familiar with the full range of philosophy may view it as having a morbid preoccupation with human suffering, injustice, and death; with attacking ideas that may lift us up such as religion and mysticism. Admittedly, those concerns are voiced by philosophers, but they go beyond such foci to ask probing questions about the nature of man and reality, the ethical foundations of a good life, and the social foundations of a good community. Certainly, they have little patience with nonsense and weak arguments. But they do emerge from the shadows of hard critique to focus on the things that matter most in human existence.

Another old friend **Mark** Twain, *Biography of Mark Twain*, shouts at me with sharp candor and painful humor as I end this review of my Philosophy library. He reminds me to enjoy the *Philosophy* section of the newspaper, more commonly known as "The Comics." Some philosophers have a playful sense of humor (as I do), and read the comics from a philosophical perspective. Doonesbury, Calvin and Hobbes, Dilbert, and Pickles are among my current favorites. It is the first section of the paper I read in the morning, not without some discussion with coffeehouse friends. Also, Thomas Cathcart and Daniel Klein two books, *Plato and a Platypus Walk into a Bar* and *Heidegger and a Hippo Walk through those Pearly Gates* used the power of humor to more fully understand philosophy with a smile. John and Donald Capps joined in with: *You've Got to Be Kidding: How Jokes Can Help You Think*. When I hear nonsense, I resist the urge to point out logical fallacies and untested assumptions, but simply respond with wit.

IX

My library, of course, grew to over three thousand volumes (home and university), and it was not limited to philosophy and science, although those were certainly the largest sections. Other sections were: Psychology; Nature and Environment; Poetry and Prose; Political Science; Economics; Leadership; and Adventure and Travel. Approximately, 250 of these authors became *friends* as cited in this essay, as many authors were simply read, faded from frequent recollection, and eventually collected dust.

Along the way, I found solace in nature related prose and poetry, and to my initial surprise, discovered philosophy between the lines, often articulating insights and emotions better, parsimoniously, albeit with intense passion, rather than analytical rigor. Some of my best *friends* along my journey of discovery in the natural world were: **Edward** Abbey, *Desert Solitaire* and *Down the River*; **David** Bower, *Let the Mountains Talk, Let the Rivers Run*; **Rachael** Carson, *Silent Spring*; Alison Deming, *Temporary Homelands: Essays on Nature, Spirit and Place*; **Paul** Hawkins, *Blessed Unrest*; Barbara Kingsolver, *Small Wonder*; **Barry** Lopez, *About This Life*; **Kathleen** Dean Moore, *Riverwalking* and *Holdfast* and *Wild Comfort*; Richard Nelson, *The Island Within*; Jay Walljasper, *All That We Share: A Field Guide to the Commons*; **Terry** Tempest Williams, *Refuge* and *An Unspoken Hunger* and *Finding Beauty in a Broken World*; and **Naomi** Klein, *This Changes Everything*. Other friends who joined me in this discovery and shared their poetry were: **Franz** Dolp, *Reflections on the Infinite*; **Ralph** Waldo Emerson, *Selected Essays and Poems*; Ruth

Gendler, *The Book of Qualities*; **James** Kavanaugh, *Walk Easy on the Earth* and *There Are Men Too Gentle to Live Among the Wolves*; **Carol** Lynn Pearson, *The Search;* **William** Stanford, *Ask Me* and *The Way It Is*; **Henry** David Thoreau, *Walden*; and **Walt** Whitman, *Leaves of Grass*.

I shared more of these volumes of poetry and nature writing with friends, in response to their pondering sojourns, than I did in sharing volumes of philosophy or psychology, fearing that the latter would generate more intellectual inertia than insight. Voices are clearly heard from the shelves of my library when I least expect them, in the midst of a busy metropolis or the bottom of a river canyon, reminding me of the things that matter most, and to resist being at the mercy of things that matter least. I often memorized their words, and carry them with me, always. They are all *old friends* indeed.

X

A large section of my library reflects my academic and professional interests, the social sciences including social psychology, organization theory and development, and leadership. Most of my university teaching focused on these domains. I developed many lifelong *friends:* **Gordon** Allport, *The Nature of Prejudice*; George Bach, *The Intimate Enemy*; **Daniel** Goleman, *Emotional Intelligence* and *Primal Leadership*; **Abraham** Maslow, *Toward a Psychology of Being* and *The Farther Reaches of Human Nature*; **Carl** Rodgers, *On Becoming a Person* and *On Personal Power*; Elliot Aronson, *The Social Animal*; Chris Argyris, *Reasoning, Learning, and Action*; Albert Bandura, *Social Learning Theory*; **Warren** Bennis, *On Becoming a Leader* and *Geeks and Geezers*; Wayne Cascio, *Applied Psychology*;

Robert Dubin, *Theory Building*; Marvin Dunnette, *Industrial and Organizational Psychology*; **William** Dyer, *Insight to Impact*; **Wendell** French, *Organization Development and Transformation*; Rensis Likert, *The Human Organization;* **Douglas** McGregor, *The Human Side of Enterprise*; **Chuck** Pyron, *On Leadership and Team Building*; Edgar Schein, *Process Consultation*; Gary Yukl, *Leadership in Organizations.*; Richard Carlson, *Don't Sweat The Small Stuff*; Rosabeth Kanter, *The Change Masters*; Heraclitus, *Fragments*; **Dan** Ariely, *Predictably Irrational*; and Charles Mee, *Playing God.*

From 1983-1988, I pursued and obtained a PhD from the University of Oregon with an extensive research focus on the social sciences, especially organizational and social psychology. I developed a lot of *friends* along the way. In 1991, I donated over 300 volumes to the University of Oregon when I moved to Portland, Oregon. Most of these books were ones that I acquired during my five-year PhD program. They focused on organization behavior (OB), social and organizational psychology, leadership, business law, statistics, and research methodology. I retained over 700 volumes related to HRM, employment and labor law, collective bargaining, risk and safety management, dispute resolution methods, and organizational culture. In 2001, I retired from business and began teaching at OSU and UO at which time I placed these books in my UO office. I referred to them in my teaching over the next fifteen years, and along the way, gave over 100 volumes to interested associates and students. In 2016, I retired from the UO and donated most of these books (approximately 500) to the UO, UO professors, or PhD students there. There are many *old friends* within these volumes who will remain unnamed in this essay, and who inspired me to write and publish (UO Press) an academic book entitled *Reinventing HRM.*

All of my *friends* have spoken to me frequently during my careers in business, research, and education, reminding me of what really matters most in engaging people. Over forty years with six business firms, I had professional success, in part because I listened to their voices. Over forty years of mostly concurrent university teaching, I used their theories and methods to enrich the education and lives of my students, in part because I listened to their voices. Over twenty years of concurrently conducting intense leadership development programs or organizational change interventions, I continue to listen to their wisdom and counsel. Now, I endeavor to reinvent myself as a writer, I listen still. And I will listen when they tell me it's time to relax and let go.

My library (both home and university) is gone now, given away in "lightening my pack" and in simplifying my life in my sunset years. It was hard to perform this task, gifting books to others, knowing that I will most likely never return to their pages again. It was a sad farewell to *friends*, I thought. However, I was wrong. I discover that they speak to me still, my mind permitting. After all, they are ***lifelong friends.***

Love

ॐ

When you
seek love
you will not
find it.

If you don't
seek love
It will
find you.

When you
withhold love
all will be
withheld.

If you
give love
all will be
given to you.

Final Reflection

ॐ

If you don't know the kind of person I am
And I don't know the kind of person you are
A pattern that others made may prevail in the world
And following the wrong god home we may miss our star.
A Ritual to Read to Each Other, William Stafford

Author's final reflection:

How do we know

who I am

who you are

the pattern others made

the wrong god

our star

How do we know

by being real

the pattern makes us less real

the wrong god is merely stuff

the star is our life.

Acknowledgments

ଓ୫

I echo the same words of praise here as I did in my first book, *Finding Heart.* This book arose because of years of support from my wife and life companion, Linda Fuss. She gave me the space to write, the encouragement to share, and a sense of purpose to celebrate. She patiently listened to me read my work and tirelessly read and edited my work. She is my dreamer, muse, and conscience.

This book also arose because of the rich heritage of philosophical engagement and storytelling in my early family, as my father, mother, grandfather, uncle, and great-aunt mentored my growth. Stories about my Hungarian heritage are mostly attributed to ones told to me by my grandfather and are retold to the best of my aging memory. No fictional details were added, though some factual assertions may be inaccurate.

I thank friends who have influenced me to become a more reflective thinker and a better writer, especially Scott, Steve, Jim, David, Peter, Rance, Tom, Lolly, Mike, Sam, Maryanne, and Jerry.

I wish to fully recognize the good humor and loving kindness of my children (Chris, Steve, and Julianne), and grandchildren (Nathan, Jacob, Leah Rose, Madeline, Steven Baily, Kody, and Max). They have patiently listened to my stories and reflections over the years.

I wish to thank my editor, Vera Haddan, for her meticulous and tireless efforts in reviewing my manuscript. Her line editing was indeed an incredible learning experience for me. I also thank my publisher, Amazon's CreateSpace and Kindle Direct Publishing, for consistently producing a high-quality volume.

About the Author

☙

Steven J. Mayer is mostly an armchair philosopher in his sunset years, enjoying a simple life in a beautiful place with the beautiful woman in his life. His education and professions matter less than the amazing people who have touched his life over the years. He is slowly reinventing himself as a writer, when he is not walking the beach, enjoying his family, pursuing adventures, or traveling to the ends of the earth.

Made in the USA
Columbia, SC
06 September 2022

66111383R00178